GOOD DESIGN CAN CHANGE YOUR LIFE

Also by Ty Pennington

Ty's Tricks

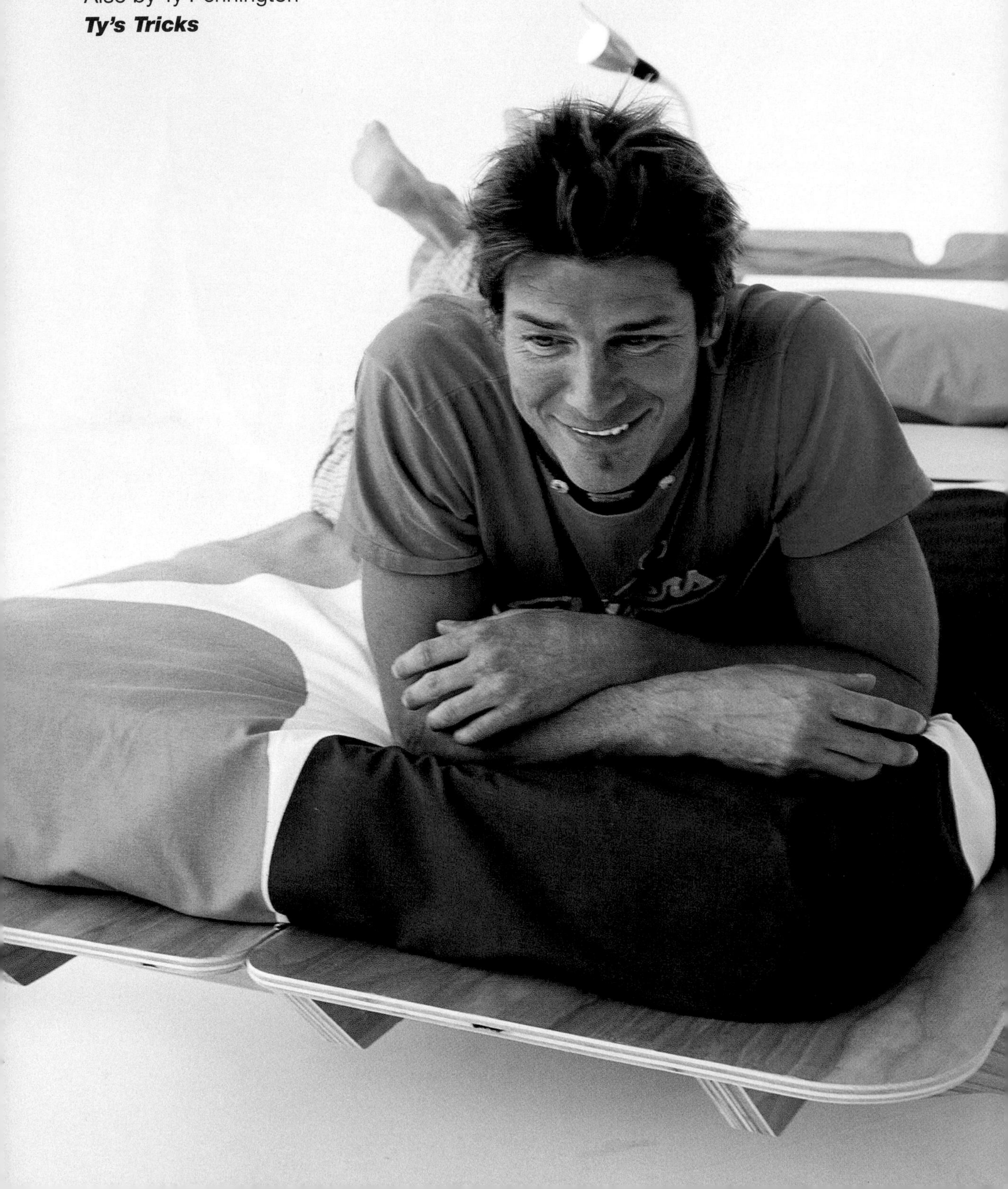

TY PENNINGTON

GOOD DESIGN CAN CHANGE YOUR LIFE

Beautiful Rooms, Inspiring Stories

Simon & Schuster Paperbacks
New York   London   Toronto   Sydney

Simon & Schuster Paperbacks
A Division of Simon & Schuster, Inc.
1230 Avenue of the Americas
New York, NY 10020

First Simon & Schuster trade paperback edition
September 2008

SIMON & SCHUSTER PAPERBACKS and
colophon are registered trademarks of Simon &
Schuster, Inc.

For information about special discounts for bulk
purchases, please contact Simon & Schuster
Special Sales at 1-800-456-6798 or business@
simonandschuster.com

Designed by Ruba Abu-Nimah & Eleanor Rogers

Manufactured in the United States of America

10   9   8   7   6   5   4   3   2

Library of Congress Cataloging-in-Publication Data

Pennington, Ty.
Good design can change your life: beautiful rooms,
inspiring stories by Ty Pennington.
p. cm.
1. Interior decoration—Psychological aspects.
I. Title.
NK2113.P46 2008
747—dc22
ISBN-13: 978-0-7432-9474-4
ISBN-10:   0-7432-9474-2

Acknowledgments

This book is dedicated to all the families that have opened up their hearts and their homes and trusted me with their stories as well as their most private spaces. I was truly honored to be able to give them not only my creativity, but a new look at themselves, a new start, something to be proud of and, sometimes, a place to heal. The reward for me was in seeing their reactions, screams and tears of joy! I think I might have the greatest job in the world. I absolutely love it. From the first sketch to the finished product, it's quite a process and a lot of hard work. And I couldn't do it alone.

I know I am a bit of a control freak, but its only because I want things to be the best that they can be. Yet, for me at least, all that chaos is fun because I get to go through it with my friends, my team. And they are the best. . . .

First and foremost this book would never have gotten done if not for Drea, my girl, my love, my friend. I work all the time, and when I am not working I am thinking about what I should be working on next. It's ironic that my job is designing and bringing people home, yet I rarely ever get to be at our home. It's hard and I can never thank you enough for your patience and dedication. They broke the mold when they made you. You make the world a better place to be.

There are so many others who help me "make it happen." I have to give it up to "my man" Bill Stankey, for your wisdom, honor, honesty, but most of all for your ability to be a loyal human being in a sea of sharks. Thanks to Marc Chamlin for your expertise and eye for detail. It's priceless. Thanks also to Stan Rosenfield, you're the best. Of course, I couldn't forget the people who made it possible for me to be where I am today. Leigh Seaman, you opened the door of opportunity and never let it close. Thank you for believing in me back then and for your friendship and brilliance now. Thanks to the hardest working executive producer in television, Denise Cramsey. Through a sea of confusion and chaos, you can find not only the truth and human spirit, but also, most importantly, the way home. I'd also like to thank Daryn Eller for all of your patience and hard work. I know it was tough. To my family and friends, Craig Bailey, Rob Williams, and Nancy Hadley, thanks for all that you do. To David Goldberg, thanks for taking a chance on me. And finally, thank you to my crew Team Alpha and Bravo. You guys are the hardest working, most fun-loving human beings I have ever worked with. It's an honor!!!!!!

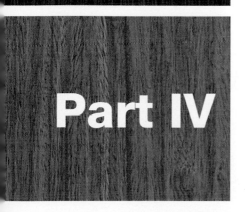
Part I

Part II

Part III

Part IV

Introduction

Imagine that one day you inexplicably find yourself living in an extremely bad situation. Your house is in shambles, run-down inside and out, the yard choked with weeds. You've tried to fix things up, but, frankly, you've got more pressing things on your mind, including a young daughter battling cancer, a wedding ring pawned to help pay her medical expenses, and long hours at a grocery store job trying to make ends meet. Then, just as it seems almost too much to bear, you hear a very loud and annoying voice yelling your family's name through a megaphone. The next thing you know, you and your family are being whisked away for a much-needed week's vacation, while a group of TV people stick around to spruce up your house. "Cool," you think, "it'll be nice to have a room or two redecorated."

Well, not exactly.

That family—featured on the very first episode of *Extreme Makeover: Home Edition*—was more than a little surprised to come home to a whole new house, not just a few revamped rooms. Now, of course, people know what to expect when they hear me shouting "Good morning!" outside their door. But that initial makeover was a revelation to everyone involved, including me—and I'm not talking just about the sheer amount of people power that went into the job (though that was pretty amazing, too). While I'd been crafting furniture, designing rooms, and renovating homes for years, until I began my job as team leader on *EMHE*, I don't think I realized how much difference having a comfortable, well-designed, and beautiful place to live can make in someone's life. Sure, I've always been passionate about houses, but the experience of creating warm, inviting sanctuaries for families who really need them has made me a true believer in the power of positive rethinking. If you want to inject light, energy, and optimism into your life, making over your home—or even just a single room—is a good place to start.

I know for sure that the instant that first *EMHE* family walked into their new house, their lives had changed for the better. I don't think any of us, including all the neighbors and community members who had come out to help us, were quite prepared for how dramatic and emotional that moment would be. When the first show aired, my brother called. "Dude," he said, "there's not a dry eye in America right now." I was crying, too, even though I was seeing the episode a second time, so the conversation was a little awkward. How, I was wondering, did I get lucky enough to get this job, the greatest, most rewarding experience of my life? And who would have thought years ago, when I was a kid drawing on the walls, breaking furniture, and pretty much destroying my family's home, that I would someday be destroying and rebuilding strangers' homes and being thanked rather than sent to my room.

You don't need to have had bad luck or a tragedy in your life to be in need of a big or even a little change on the home front. We all need change. Change is good, and that's especially true when it comes to the rooms where you've spent a good portion of your life. I'll even go as far as to say that making changes in your home can completely change your life. Think about it. When you wake up in the morning, the first thing you see when you open your eyes is your bedroom. Does that make you happy or does it only remind you of how much crap you've got piled up and need to find a place for? Either way, it's got to affect your outlook for the day. How ready will you be to tackle the day's challenges if your first sight reminds you of how you've neglected your house? And how cheery are you going to be when you step out to greet your kids, your significant other, your dog, or whoever if the state of your living quarters has already put you in a bad mood?

Likewise when you come home at the end of a day. If everything is the same as it's been for years and years—and not comforting-same, but depressing-same—your home will seem stale and, by extension, so might your life. Yet if you've taken the time to put some soul and feeling into your décor, things might seem quite the opposite. And the alterations don't

even have to be major—a gallon of paint goes a long way. It doesn't matter if you own or rent where you live, it's your nest, your habitat—it's you. Make it an inviting, fun, and relaxing place to come home to.

The key is to design rooms that reflect what you're all about. Your home should be a place with colors, textures, sights, smells, and sounds that please you. It should be completely personal, the palace you've always wanted to live in—even if it's just a mini version of that lavish pad you pictured. No matter that you can't afford the Taj Mahal; you can have the Garage Mahal! As long as the rooms are suited to you, it's going to be great.

Changing your home makes you feel like you have a chance to start over. Change begets change. Change the look of your living room and maybe you'll look at the world differently. Change your bedroom and maybe you'll begin to get a different idea of your future and what you want to accomplish. Every week on *EMHE* we give people a fresh start in their homes, and it so often translates into a fresh start in life. One thing I'm certain of is that a home is so much more than the place where you eat and sleep. It is—or it should be—a reflection of all the things that matter to you.

What most people need to initiate change is inspiration. I hope that you've watched *EMHE* and thought, "Yeah, my house could use a change, too." What you probably don't know, though, is that there is a lot more inspiration to be gleaned from what we do on the show that never even makes it into the one-hour broadcast. That's why part of the mission

behind this book is to give you more of the inside scoop on what goes into each project as well as an insider's view of "Ty's secret rooms," the rooms that I personally create for families. I want to share my passion for intelligent, imaginative design and let you in on all the tricks for crafting unique, personal interiors that I've learned down (sometimes literally) in the trenches. By the end of this book, you'll know exactly what it takes, from Step A to Step Z, to bring a little more style into your life.

Unless you have the ABC network and your entire town standing by with a wrecking ball, it's easier and far more affordable to tackle one or a few rooms at a time, so I've narrowed this book down to three high-impact areas of the house: bedrooms, living spaces, and work spaces. I'm also going to talk about the elements of style that apply to all rooms, including

what to look at before you leap (what stays, what goes, how to make a floor plan); how to decide what style you're going to go for; and how to use color and texture in ways that are unexpected, but not insane. You don't want it to look like you got inspiration from a clown college (though maybe Bozo Bohemian is your thing, which is fine by me).

I also want to encourage you and give you the nail-by-nail instructions on how to build some of your own furnishings. The TV audience might not know it, but I design custom furniture for just about every room I do on the show. Someone else usually builds it for me now only because the show's time crunch makes it impossible to build it myself. But I've handcrafted hundreds of different pieces over the years and I still love it. The great thing about building your own furniture and accessories is that it's not

terribly difficult and it's so gratifying to know that you've created a major design element (or even a minor one) for your home with your bare hands. Your friends will be pretty impressed, too. Really. You've got to try it.

Keep in mind that you don't have to overhaul a room completely to give it a striking makeover. Sometimes fooling around with just one or two elements is all you need to do. My goal here is to give you tons of ideas from which you can pick and choose. We'll talk about walls and floors, lighting and storage, wallpaper and fabric—yes, *I'm* going to talk

about wallpaper and fabric. This might seem slightly weird if you, like most people, think of me as just a nail-and-hammer guy. I am a nail-and-hammer guy, but I have an extensive background in art and design, and they're my passion. Wow, did I just say the word *passion*? Didn't expect that either, did you?

When I was a kid growing up in Atlanta, the only way my mom could get me to sit still and focus on anything was when she gave me a sketchpad or some kind of art project to work on. Otherwise, I was wreaking havoc, unscrewing the legs of the piano, drawing a picture on the wall with crayons—why not?—and basically redesigning the house. I wasn't much better in school. I definitely had some issues with conduct and, being who I am, a lot of excess energy. So I caused chaos in the classroom, climbing in and out of windows, slapping Johnny on the back of the head. As it happens, my mom was studying to be a child psychologist and, as part of her course work, she came to my elementary school and asked to study the worst kid in the school. Who do you think was sent to the front? Oh yeah, it all made for some interesting school and family dynamics.

But I wasn't completely hopeless. I had some trouble studying, but I found that I could do well if I had a visual frame of reference. I was good at geometry, for instance, because it involved shapes and putting things together. And I found that I could memorize facts for history class if I drew little pictures of battle scenes or whatever event was in the curriculum. Approaching information visually made all the difference for me—and it still does.

I always wanted to be an artist, but my parents were a little skeptical about the idea, since it's not the easiest route to a solid bank account. So I figured out that I could go to art school to become a graphic designer, which might land me a legitimate job. It turned out that I loved it. I loved it so much that when I was asked to do one project, I'd do three. (I was a real overachiever beaver on that one.) I also started doing carpentry, working on building houses, but I never thought of it as a future vocation; it was just a way to pay for school.

After I graduated, I got a job at a graphic design studio and won some design awards while continuing to study painting and sculpture. It was all going well, but not long into it, I met a model scout who encouraged me to try modeling. The pay, he promised, would be great. So, even though I had hilariously long hair with a kind of funky rat tail in the back, I went into the modeling agency office. A week later I was on a plane to Japan and entering what would become my wanderlust phase. Modeling gave me the travel bug and opened new worlds for me. I had never been anywhere. Now I was going to Europe and Asia and living in New York City, Japan, Thailand, and Italy. I wasn't exactly striking it rich by modeling, but I was seeing the world and in the process learning so much about different cultures, different religions, and different ways of life. I began to see everything, including art, architecture, and furniture, in a completely different way.

When I came back from traveling, I returned to both construction and graphic design and worked for a while on movie sets (you can actually catch me in the credits for the Nicolas Cage film *Leaving Las Vegas*). I was once again living in Atlanta and renovating a warehouse I'd bought with my brother, when I went on an audition for a cable show. The premise was that two neighbors would swap houses while we invaded and made over their homes. The producers of the show, *Trading Spaces*, were impressed when I showed them the simple trick of using a speed square to cut straight 2 × 4s and I thought, "Wow, you guys have never seen a speed square before? You definitely need a carpenter." And for four years, I was it. The carpenter guy. Ty, the handy guy.

It was the perfect job for me. I got to build things and be my off-the-wall, wiseass self in front of the camera. Every week, though, we'd wait for the family to come home to see if they were going to like what we did to their house. And sometimes they definitely did *not*—in fact, some people came home and cried. The shock value was a lot of fun, but I also thought it would be great to do a show where we do something for people who need help and who actually like what we do. I thought, "Why not cry for the *right* reason?"

Enter *Extreme Makeover: Home Edition*. The producers asked me, "Do you think we can build a house in seven days?" and I said, "No, but it would definitely be good television to try." And so we did, and it's been an absolutely amazing ride. During that first episode, when an entire community, not to mention a couple hundred construction workers, five designers, and a production staff came together

to make something incredible happen in one week, I thought, "I don't know how well this is going to play on television, but I know that I have to do this again."

The years I've spent working on *EMHE* as well as on my other "job"—designing a line of home fashions for Sears—have helped me refine my ideas about what constitutes good design. More than anything, I think, good design artfully brings together practicality and emotion. It allows you to capture a mood—and that mood could be transcendental calm in, say, a bedroom or maybe wicked crazy fun in an entertainment room—without losing sight of the room's real purpose.

With this book, I hope to get you to look at your home with fresh eyes and contemplate the possi-

bilities. How can you integrate the things you are passionate about—whether it's music and dance or nature or a particular culture—into the look of your home? How do you grab elements from a particular style and make them your own? I think you'll find that it's not that hard or expensive. You're not going to have to leave the bank with a wheelbarrow in order to create a home that's stylish and intimate. You'll see. It's all incredibly doable.

And the rewards are just fantastic. Take it from someone who has had the good fortune to help all kinds of families settle into stylish homes. Revamping your own rooms is going to be uplifting. It may even change your total outlook on life.

Ten Ways to Know That Your Home Needs a Makeover

1.
You wake up and can't see the floor because clothing, books, and debris are everywhere.

2.
You can't open the door of the closet because you've shoved so many things into it.

3.
You're using plastic storage bins as dresser drawers and milk crates as furniture.

4.
You've made shelving out of cinderblocks and 1 x 12s.

5.
Your clothes are in garbage bags or in boxes still labeled "Closet."

6.
You're sleeping on the floor with the moving blanket that you still have from when you first moved in.

7.
There's absolutely no artwork up except pizza boxes.

8.
There are no blinds on your window, and the first thing that hits you in the morning is the bright sun, shining like a laser.

9.
You're lying in bed, a bus goes by, and your whole house rattles and rolls, then a little bit of drywall falls off the ceiling and hits you on the head. (I speak from experience.)

10.
It's the holidays, the family is coming to visit, and your mother-in-law or step-mom or grandparents walk in and the first thing they say is, "You know, we think we'll get a hotel room."

Part I
Prep Work

How to Plan for a Makeover

I've done many things in life without planning ahead and with little forethought. I used to get plans for home makeovers written on napkins and then try to wing it. Sometimes it would all work out. Sometimes—well, let's just say, better luck next time. Having done it both ways, I highly recommend going the premeditated game-plan route, even if you're just doing a small design renovation. **It may seem like we're flying by the seat of our pants on *EMHE*, but we actually go in with a pretty well thought-out plan.** And not with just an architectural plan, but with a design plan for each room. Not every idea ends up working, and sometimes—make that a lot of times—we have to improvise at the last minute. But we wouldn't get the results we do if we didn't map out everything beforehand.

Prepping for a makeover can be boiled down to twelve steps (not *those* twelve steps, though sometimes they can help, too). A lot of what's involved is simply looking at a room in a way that you've never looked at it before. Where are the windows? How high are the ceilings? What shape is the floor in? Make sure you've got a tape measure because you're going to write down the room's dimensions and draw up a floor plan. You've also got to take some kind of measure of yourself: your passions, your personality, your memories, your fantasies, your sense of style, what makes you feel comfortable, what kind of mood you want to set—those things will all play a role in determining what the room is going to look like. You'll love a room, even something as utilitarian as an office, so much more if you put your heart and soul into it.

Start with a Style Folder

I'm always working. Even when I'm not involved in a specific project, I'm keeping an eye out for things I like: layouts from home décor magazines, pages from art and design books, fabric swatches, samples of colors and textures I dig, photographs of clothes with patterns that look great, brochures from hotels, snapshots of rooms, signs, art, restaurants, gardens, lobbies. I save anything that I think is awesome-looking and that might serve as design inspiration at some point. (I also collect airsickness bags from planes, but that's another story.) When it comes to redoing a room, there's one word I can't reiterate enough: research, research, research.

Just to stay organized, I file everything in a "style folder." You don't have to create a style folder with one particular project in mind—simply collect things you admire with the hope that they'll one day be useful. If you just toss in everything that catches your eye, you'll probably see a certain look start to emerge. You might not have been aware that you were drawn to certain colors, patterns, or types of furniture.

Magazines are a great place to start. If you have your own subscription, you can just rip out the pages and file them away without having to save stacks and stacks of issues. Also look at as many home design books as possible. When the costs get prohibitive, see what your library has on hand (and if its selection is small, see if they can borrow from other branches).

When you're saving things, though, don't think only about pictures; think about texture, too. Start touching things. Feel the difference between linen and Egyptian cotton, burlap and velour, and

whenever you can toss samples of textures you like into your style folder, do so. (It would probably be bad form to shear off a piece of the bedspread in your cousin's guest room, so just write down the fabric type and what you liked about it then tuck that note into your folder.)

There are a lot of ways to make a style folder. You can dump everything into an accordion folder. I like to take photos of everything from fabrics to magazine spreads with my digital camera and upload them onto my computer. (You can also scan things directly into your computer and skip the photographing part.) This lets me organize everything into files on my desktop, print out whatever I want, and take it with me when I need to. Just remember to back up your hard drive. That's a lesson I don't want to learn again. Fixing them is *hard* and it will *drive* you crazy. Good times!

The Twelve Steps

Making over a room can be a messy job and I'm not just talking about the paint, dust, stray bolts and nails, and all that other stuff that gets all over the floor. I mean that there's a mess of things you have to think about and a mess of ideas you have to juggle. It's easy to forget things or make mistakes. Sometimes mistakes are no big deal, and in fact, you can even end up going in a different and better direction because of a mistake. But more often mistakes are costly or, at the very least, frustrating, so try to avoid them from the start.

Because of the intense nature of *EMHE*, and, let's be honest, the intense nature of *me*, I probably seem like I'm all over the place on TV. But I'm actually a pretty methodical guy and this is one place—the planning stage—where being methodical definitely pays off. That's what these twelve steps are for. Think of them as your guide to getting organized (and preventing future screwups). And here's a tip: Write down everything. Don't risk letting any of the good ideas running through your head get lost in the ether. And make sure you can read your own handwriting. Hieroglyphics are even more confusing.

1.
Snap a Photo

Take a "before" picture of the room. You'll want to remember it the way it was because it's going to be oh so much better! Okay, now you only have eleven more steps to go.

2.
Assess What You Like and What You Don't Like

Make two lists: one for what you like about the room and one for what you don't like. This is just to get a general sense of what needs to change. The furniture? The wall colors? The window treatments? The floor? Now is the time to consider whether you can live with the shag carpeting left behind by the former owner or if it's time to put in hardwood floors and a few throw rugs.

Walk around the room and look at its construction. Are there any awkward spaces? Does the room have symmetry or are the windows and doors out of balance? Before you can decide on the specific changes you want to make, get a read on the big picture. What is the purpose of each room, and what about that room is and isn't working now?

3.
Save Four Things

Choose four things that you want to keep when you make over the room. There are probably a few items that still appeal to you or that you feel you just can't let go of. It might be a piece of furniture, a work of art, a rug, a lamp. If you've got to be crazy, go ahead and pick six. But here's the thing. Sometimes people have a tough time getting rid of stuff that they've had forever. But if it doesn't have sentimental value and it wasn't handed down by a grandparent or an uncle

OPPOSITE PAGE Can this chair be saved? A little reupholstering should do the trick.

You've Got to Have Friends: Throw a Makeover Party

One of my first major design-and-build projects was a three-story tree house (with a sundeck) that I created in my backyard when I was eleven years old.

To get other kids in the neighborhood to work on it with me—kids whose dads had better tools than mine—I took a page from Tom Sawyer and bartered, trading comic books for their help. I remember the bond I felt with those kids while we built that tree house together, and it's the same feeling I get today working with not only the *EMHE* team, but also the hundreds of local contractors and volunteers that help us do our job. I like to have as much fun as possible when I'm working, and I've found that bringing in a

crowd to help makes a project livelier and even gets you better results. You never know what ideas someone else is going to bring to the table.

So I urge you to get help on your makeover, but in order to do that you've got to make people *want* to come over, and that's where a makeover party comes in. The promise of music, food, drink, and a good time makes people forget that you'd also like them to do a little heavy lifting, hammering, and painting. To me, food and drink is important, but music is the key thing. Make sure you have a CD player or some other kind of sound system to keep everyone's energy up. You can even create a makeover-inspired CD for the occasion,

though if your friends are very literal (and unless you're going for the Goth look) avoid adding songs like "Paint It Black" by the Rolling Stones. And, hey, if you have a megaphone, absolutely pull it out! I can say from experience that making as much noise as possible gets people fired up to do a job well. If you don't want to gather a whole group of friends, call on one or two and swap something for their help. Cook them a great meal, let them use your boat or car, help them make over their own homes the following weekend. Just repay them in some way so that you can really put them to work and not feel guilty about it.

There's also no reason you can't take a page from *Extreme*

Makeover: Home Edition's book and get a group together to work on a project for someone who you know is in need of help. Maybe you have a sick friend or relative, or you know someone who has just gone through a crisis like divorce or the death of a family member. Create a surprise for that person by making over one or more of her rooms with or without her knowing; the pleasure she (or he) takes in the result will be one of the most fantastic rewards you've ever received.

And if you do it right, the project can be a blast. A few years ago I designed a mural for a bedroom belonging to a family in Colorado that had adopted several troubled foster kids destined for juvenile hall or prison. The

mural (you can see it on pages 114 and 115) was a very detailed rendering of a bandana-type pattern, in keeping with the fact that the house was on a ranch and the parents were horse whisperers. I had to project the pattern on the wall, pencil it in, then go back and paint each individual shape, some of which were only one to two inches long. Fortunately, a family of five that had been helping out with the whole makeover project as well as my friend Nancy, a muralist, ended up pitching in. It took us *nine* hours, but it was such a good time. We listened to music and chowed down on pizza while watching this beautiful pattern take shape throughout the night. It was great fun and well worth the effort.

Here's another makeover party idea for you. If you're low on funds for your makeover project but rich in stuff that you'd like to get rid of, have a Raffle for Renovation party. Invite a lot of people, offer music and drink, and sell tickets for a couple of bucks. Before my TV days, I threw one of these parties and unloaded a ton of things that had been piling up in my garage. I threw in some bikes and an old car that didn't run anymore. You can even throw in things that have no value like a bucket of bricks, just for the fun of it. By the end of the night you get rid of all that stuff you'd been collecting for years, and you also made a pretty good chunk of change that you can put toward your makeover project.

ABOVE Kitchen cabinet: Getting feedback on your design ideas is invaluable. Here's me at home brainstorming with the team from Sears.

or somebody very special and you're just hanging on to it because you always have, ask yourself, Is it really going to work in the new room I'll be creating? Are you just leaving it there because it's easier to shove stuff into it or pile stuff on top of it than to figure out how to organize the room more intelligently? If you really have no good reason to hang on to something, let it go. Like an old boyfriend or girlfriend you thought you could never live without, you probably won't miss it much after, well, a few months.

4.
Remove Everything Else

Sweep the room clean so that it's an empty canvas. If this is too much of an ordeal (say, you've got a three-hundred-pound armoire that you aren't going to

want to move more than once), at least remove all the knickknacks, art, window coverings, light furniture, and rugs so that the room is as bare as possible. In other words, strip it naked. It's time to hose it down and clean behind the ears (or the nightstand).

5.
Look at the Room in an Entirely New Way

When you look at a room that's familiar, it's hard to see what's really there. That's why I suggest taking everything (or almost everything) out even if it means you have to move it all back in again before you actually get to work. Then once the room is clear, think about how it might work differently. Take a look at how much space you actually have. Notice the ceiling height. If it's low, you should keep your furniture somewhat low, too, otherwise the furniture is going to make the room seem small. A platform bed, for instance, works perfectly in a bedroom with low eight-foot ceilings. (See "Big Ideas for Small Spaces," page 15 for more tips.) If it's high, you'll have room for taller pieces—things like a four-poster bed and really high curtains.

Next, look to see if the room is naturally well balanced. Symmetry and balance make a room feel like it's working. Not everything has to be so cookie-cutter perfect that if you cut a room in half each side would match, but there should be some equilibrium so that the room doesn't have all the detail or large features on one side. (If you need an example, look no further than the bedroom: That's the reason we have lamps on both sides of the bed.) If symmetry isn't built into the room, you may need to choose your furnishings to create it. Balance is a little tricky to describe, but you'll know it when you see it. Say, for instance, that there is a window to the left of the spot where you want to place your couch, but no window to the right. Instead of placing two end tables and lamps on either side of the couch as you might normally do, maybe you just need to opt for an end table and lamp on the right side to balance out the window. These are the kinds of things to think about before you choose your furnishings.

While you're surveying the room, check out whether there is any space that was previously wasted. Was there some awkward area (usually wall space) in the room's previous incarnation that you never knew what to do with? Think about how you might use this space. Can you add shelving or put up an entertainment center? Hang a piece of art or put up picture ledges for displaying photos? Carve out a cubbyhole in the wall where you can display something meaningful to you or turn it into an indoor "window" that lets light into the next room?

Now think about what the room is really used for. If it's a bedroom, maybe you only sleep there, but maybe you also use it as a place to watch TV or read.

Maybe it's the room where the whole family hangs out. Living rooms, in particular, get used for so many different things. Some are primarily for entertaining. Some are the site for all music and movie enjoyment. Some are game rooms. Offices generally have one purpose—work—however, what kind of work will you be doing in there? And what kinds of work paraphernalia will you need to store there? Lots of books, files, notebooks, photographs? Figuring out the room's most important function is going to help you furnish it well and lay it out properly. You don't want to end up with a dysfunctional room.

6.
Check Out the State of Your Walls, Floors, and Ceilings

Are they in good shape or do they need repair? Before you can figure out how much you'll need to spend and how much time you're going to put into this project, you need to know if repair work is called for. If it is, it's going to be the first thing you attend to because you want to start with a perfectly blank slate. Walls in particular take a lot of wear and tear. You have a couple of friends over for the holidays, people get fired up, and you know who suffers? The walls. They get nicked and kicked. And that's not even counting all the marks furniture leaves and, if you've got young kids who are as inspired as I once was, smudges from markers and crayons. Most walls need to be spackled and sanded, though if they're really damaged, you might even have to replace the drywall. Ceilings don't tend to have as many problems unless you've had a leak. If you've got a drop ceiling with stains, you might think about replacing the whole thing. At the very least, replace any discolored tiles.

And what about the floors? When you get out of bed barefoot, do you like what you're stepping on? Is it old flooring that needs to be refinished? Is it really bad, disgusting carpet with stains? Sometimes you get a place that somebody else lived in and, well, they had animals and not very well trained animals at that. You probably just need to rip that thing out and start over. (Especially if you have pets yourself. Even animal trainers can't stop animals from getting wind of the old scent and marking their territory.)

7.
Decide What Furniture You Need That You Don't Already Have

You've figured out what you want to get rid of, now think about what you want to replace it with. If your resources are limited, I suggest that you focus on getting one great piece of furniture, determined by which piece it is that you will use and look at most. If you're choosing something for a communal space, maybe it's an entertainment center because that's what you're using the room for. If it's for your bedroom, it might be the bed; for an office, the desk. Now's also the time to contemplate building some stuff on your own. As I've said, I'm a big believer in doing it yourself, and there are several pieces that are easy to make (see appendix). Also, when you build some of the furniture yourself, you can make pieces that harmonize with everything else in the room. It'll save you from having to drag from one store or flea market to another looking for something that goes with the great couch or bed you just invested in.

8.
Check the Lighting, Both During the Day and at Night

The amount and type of light affects the mood of the room. To me, a big overhead light in the center of the room is dull—it makes everything in the room (including the people) look drab and unattractive. On the other hand, accent lighting—like table and floor lamps, sconces, directional lights you can aim at the walls—warms up everything. To get a sense of what you're going to need, look at the space you have available and think about what in the room you literally want to spotlight and where you need light for practical reasons (e.g., for reading).

Also consider how much you want to spend—lamps are generally the least expensive form of lighting because you don't need to get an electrician involved—and what lights will need to have three-way bulbs or dimmers. I highly recommend anything that lets you control light brightness and direction because there will be times when you want to soften the light. If, for instance, you sleep with someone who doesn't read as much as you do in bed, putting a three-way bulb in your bedside lamp or installing a sconce that swings out and lets you direct the light right over your book will allow your significant other the luxury of lying in bed without being blinded. Or let's say you're a single guy and you're trying to get closer to your lady. You've got sexy music cranking on the stereo, then you switch on the light, and suddenly you've gone from Barry White to Very Bright. It's a mood killer.

It's also important to get a read on how much natural light the room gets during the day. The more natural light you have permeating a room, the more joy and happiness the room will radiate. Use daylight as one decisive factor in selecting your window treatments. If the room isn't particularly light, you don't want heavy shades, blinds, or curtains that will diminish it further. Yet you don't want to lose all sense of privacy. There are a lot of different shades designed to deal with this dual problem, some of which are made of synthetic mesh that lets light filter through while blocking prying eyes. You can also get bottom-up shades that allow the sun to shine in at the top while providing coverage at the bottom.

There are ways to get creative with this, too. Instead of putting up window treatments in my old house in Atlanta, I created shoji-like screens out of white Plexiglas and placed them in front of the windows. They let in light but blocked out my neighbor's backyard. I also planted bamboo outside the window, which created wonderful shadows on the screens.

If you're going to redo the room on a pretty big scale and you don't think it has enough light, you might even think about making some structural changes. Add another window or a skylight if possible. Or you can actually cut a space—a square, a rectangle, a circle, an arched rectangle, any shape really—into one of the walls to let in light from another room. It can require having to move some of the electrical, but if you get lucky, you'll miss it and you won't have to move anything. This will not only make the room brighter, it will open it up a bit so that it seems to have more space than it actually does. And that's always a plus.

9.
Fantasize About What Your Dream Room Will Look Like

Close your eyes and picture the room you've always wanted. Does it have swaying fabric hanging from a bed or a clean-lined headboard? Does it have a cushy couch or minimalist chairs and an angular coffee table? Is it filled with books or art? Is the floor bare or covered with a soft rug? Maybe it's reminiscent of someplace you saw while on vacation or in a design book. Is it a room that's all about luxury, light, earthiness? Do you want it to be as simple as, say, brown leather chairs surrounded by white walls or as elaborate as a room filled with carved furniture and Indian tapestries? Is it a room you remember walking into as a child and thinking, "I want that room when I grow up"?

Also think about what you want it to feel like, literally. Do you want to sink into soft, cushy fabrics, or do you like the feel of fabrics that are taut and sleek? Visualize absolutely everything about the room, including how you'd like it to smell. Fantasize, too, about breaking your old habits and traditions. If you've always gone for country, visualize what it would be like to have rooms that are contemporary. The options are limited only by your imagination.

10.
Choose the Mood You Want to Set

Now that you've let your imagination run wild, rein it back in a bit and think about how to meld your fantasy with reality. The colors and the style you choose are going to help you create a mood. And you can use your fantasy to decide what that mood should be.

In the following chapters, I talk about finding your inspiration, choosing colors, and determining your style in depth. Reading those sections will help you get through this step. Basically what you want to decide here is how you want the room you're redoing to make you feel. You might, for instance, want your bedroom to be a place that relaxes you while you might want your living room to be an environment that evokes out-and-out fun. In a work space, you might want to create an area that is serene with little to distract you so that you can concentrate on the work at hand.

Color helps dictate ambiance, but so does the style of a room. Whether you're partial to mid-century modern, or you love Victorian furniture, or you want to pay homage to a particular ethnic culture, think about whether that type of décor will evoke the mood you want—or whether it can be tweaked or mixed

Big Ideas for Small Spaces

Space is the ultimate frontier. Who doesn't want more of it? I've lived in Japan where space is at a premium, as well as in tiny dorm rooms, and in overpriced, underspaced NYC apartments so I don't take a millimeter of free space for granted. And neither should you. Space makes you feel like you have room to grow, so don't box yourself in, even if it means that you don't get to put everything you want into a room.

The first design rule of thumb for a small room is to scale your furniture. Personally, I'm not a fan of big, soft, fluffy furniture to begin with. Especially big, soft, fluffy sofas: Sit down in one and you end up getting sucked into it, then the next thing you know you're totally enveloped in pillows, which is comfy but can put you to sleep in seconds, and I like to try to stay awake most of the day. If you do like big, soft, fluffy furniture, fine—just don't overstuff a small room with it or you're not going to have any space to walk around. Try to limit it to one fluffy comfortable chair or maybe just a fluffy ottoman. Or, if it's a bedroom, keep all the furnishings and the bed itself fairly streamlined and top the bed with a big fluffy comforter and pillows.

Better yet, get furniture that's sleek and low to the ground. Also consider having a few pieces on the sidelines—say, tucked away in a corner or pushed up against a wall—that you move to the center only when you have guests over. Those pieces might be stools for extra seating or even a couple of side tables that nest inside each other and can be pulled out for a cocktail party or the Super Bowl. You've got to have somewhere to put the chips, right?

If you're creating an entertainment room, also think about housing your electronic equipment in the most streamlined way possible. For instance, in my entertainment room (page 141), instead of putting my TV and stereo in a bulky cabinet or armoire, I built low, simple shelving on the wall with some little drawers and narrow shelves for storage and display. It makes the room feel more open, doesn't take up much floor space, and yet still has a decorative feel.

Probably the most important thing to remember about designing a small space is, keep it simple. Choose a few wonderful things for the room and leave it at that. Think quality, not quantity.

up with other styles to produce the atmosphere you desire. Keep in mind that a whole room doesn't have to adhere to one particular style. Mixing styles can be a great way to create an environment that's personal and unique.

11.
Compare Your Dream Room with Your Real-Life Budget and Capabilities

Okay, you've decided what you want to do. Now, how does that square with what you can realistically afford—in both time and money? Here's where you need to ask yourself how much of the work you need to hire out and how much you can do yourself. Or, how much can you ask your friends to help with. I suggest that you do get help and make kind of a party out of it. Call up a bunch of friends and say, "Hey, let's have fun this weekend. Let's get a few pizzas or whatever and make over a room." You'll be amazed at how many people will say, "That sounds like fun." The great thing is, you take advantage of your friends—of course, you'll pay them back later when they start calling, and trust me, they will—who will undoubtedly bring their own ideas to the table. And the more ideas, the better.

Friends or no friends, though, cost is still an issue. And if you can't afford to make over a room entirely, think about what parts of your dream room you *can* swing. Keep in mind that you don't need to replace absolutely everything in a room to give it new life. Sometimes when people can't afford a complete redo, they don't do anything at all, but I think it's far better to make even a few small changes. Painting a wall, adding one new piece of furniture, changing the art in the room, replacing the lighting, tossing a rug on the floor, getting different window shades—these are all easy fixes and none is very costly. (Especially the art part. You can make art out of just about anything.)

Unless you're doing some structural work that entails breaking through walls, furniture will probably be your biggest expense. But it depends on which way you want to go. There's the cheap-but-chic route, which lets you buy cool-looking furniture knowing that it's going to have a relatively short lifespan. For some people this is ideal, either because you get tired of stuff quickly or you're just in an unsettled phase of life. Then there's the high-quality and higher-priced route, where you look at furniture, new or antique, as an investment. You want something that's going to be around long enough that you can pass it on to your grandchildren. Or there's the build-it-yourself plan, which puts you somewhere in the middle costwise and lets you end up with some great one-of-a-kind pieces you can take pride in. Finally, there's the scavenger approach—searching out previously owned but good-quality furniture at garage sales, flea markets, thrift shops, on Craig's List and on eBay.

You don't, of course, have to choose only one way to go. I think some of the best rooms have a mix of furniture styles. What makes it work is that the furniture is in complementary tones and shapes, and the fabrics' colors and patterns harmonize. Personally, I tend to favor a combination of the build-it-yourself and scavenger approaches. I've made a lot of the pieces in my house, but some of them also come from thrift shops and unexpected places. I bought the chairs in my dining room, for instance, from a college that was selling off some of its old furniture (see page 143). They're a mix of primary colors, made of chrome and plastic, and I paid only five dollars for each. I put the chairs around a bright white table, which has a base I got from a flea market and a top that I built myself.

Step Eleven is the most complicated step because it may entail going back to square one and going through the steps again with a less ambitious plan. In fact, most makeovers require revising the plan more than a few times. Just know that you're going to freak out, but that you'll refigure everything and it will all work out in the end. I do it every week.

12.
Create a Floor Plan

Now you're going to commit your ideas to paper by re-creating the room in miniature so that you can play with all the elements. First, though, you need measurements. A lot of them.

Measure absolutely *everything*. Measure the floor, walls, and doors. Measure the height and width of the windows and, if you're going to be using shades, measure the inside of the window frames. Measure how high the ceilings are. Then measure all the furniture that you plan to bring back into the room. All this measuring is going to help you in two ways. First, it's going to allow you to draw up an accurate floor plan, and second, it's going to help you avoid ordering curtains that are too short or shades that don't fit in your window. Rely on only your eyes to assess dimensions and you're liable to end up with a dresser that covers part of the window or a desk that blocks a closet door. So get out the tape measure,

write down all the measurements, and keep them accessible so that when you go shopping you don't have to guess at the length of the sofa you need. (Trust me, guesstimating is aggravating—especially when you end up having to saw a sofa in half.)

When you have all your measurements written down, you'll create a floor plan. One way to do it is to find a floor plan tool online (a quick Google search will help you locate several different planning tools), then draw up your plan on your computer. If you're more of a low-tech kind of person, it's also easy to just draw a floor plan yourself. Scaling everything down (say, ½ inch = 1 foot), reproduce the room on a piece of paper. Then, on a separate piece of paper, using the same scale, draw the furnishings you have and those you anticipate purchasing (anything from beds, dressers, and entertainment centers to couches, desks, lamps, and rugs). Cut the furnishings out and try out different arrangements in the room you've drawn. This method will save you from having to draw and redraw the room a hundred times. Another

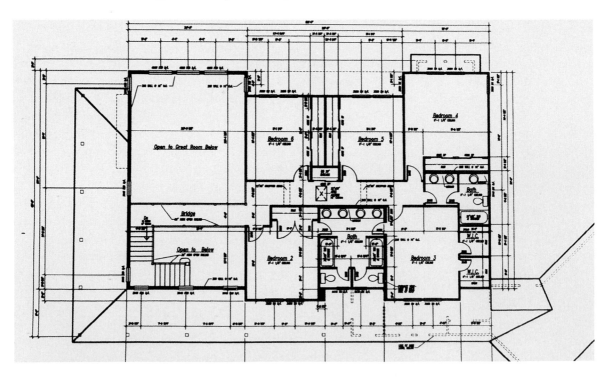

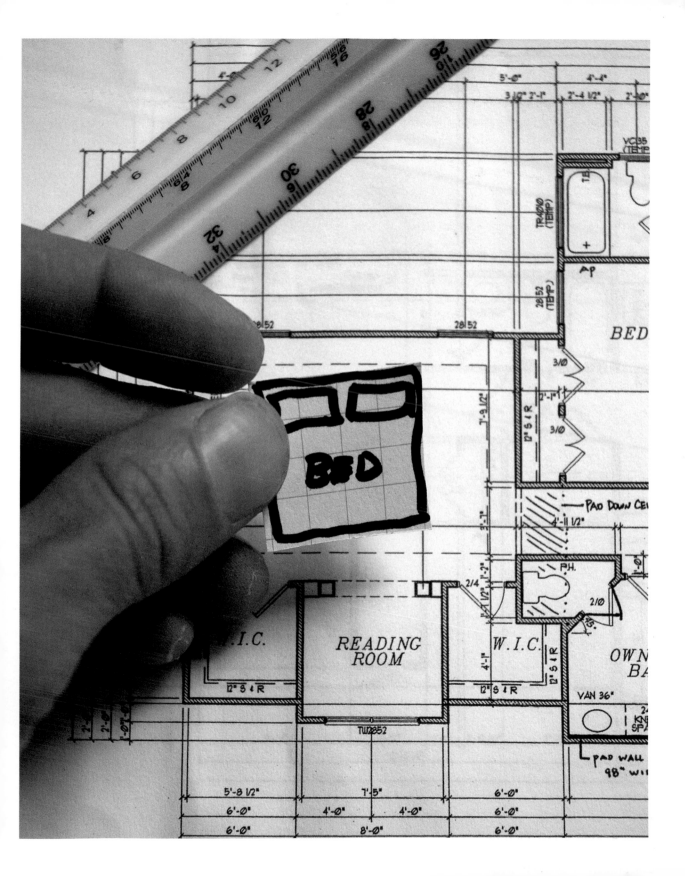

cool idea (especially if you liked building dioramas as a kid) is to take a shoebox and create a three-dimensional view of what the room could look like. You can build mini pieces of furniture out of paper or cardboard and even add paint to test out colors. Whatever way you do it, it's really worth the effort, and it's going to be a lot easier on your back than moving furniture around.

When you're making your floor plan, give some thought to creating rather than just filling space. All rooms need "flow": Open spaces make them easier to navigate as well as more open and inviting. If, for instance, you walk in through the front door of a house and are hit by the back of the couch, it kind of stops you dead in your tracks. It's like putting a Do Not Enter sign on the couch, making it harder to comfortably walk into a room and feel a part of what's going on in there. Tempting as it may be to

cram every single thing you love into a room or to opt for furniture that really doesn't fit simply because you like the style, go for spaciousness instead. Trust me. The airier the room, the less hemmed in you (and everyone else) is going to feel.

Having flow in a room also allows you to use the room for its intended purpose. One woman for whom I designed a room was a big reader with lots and lots of books. She is an inspiration. She adopted many kids, several from Russia, who nobody else would take because they had birth defects or had some other kind of disability. Because she raised them to believe in themselves, they were funny, smart, and engaging kids. She, however, had focused so much on the kids that her bedroom had become completely beside the point. She used it mostly as a study, a place to read books in between caring for the kids, which was a full-time job. As a

result, her bedroom had gotten incredibly cluttered. The bookshelves were so packed up that she was stacking books on the floor. There were also folders everywhere. Her bedroom had started functioning as an office.

My first step in designing her room was to move all the folders and many of the books out and re-create the room for the purpose it was intended: to be a place where she could relax and have some private time. Finding new places for most of the folders and books (I created the shelves on the opposite page for her so she'd still have some books on hand) freed up space for her to move and ensured that there was no mess in her line of sight (you don't have to be a neat freak to find that confronting disorder day after day is anxiety-provoking). A room that has a football field of extra space can feel cold, but one that has just the right amount of roominess and flow is perfection: It feels welcoming while still giving you space to stretch out.

Once you've made all your aesthetic decisions, you're good to go. Figure out a timeline. How long are all the changes going to take? Then develop detailed shopping and to-do lists. Your lists will depend on how much you're going to do yourself. If you're going to do a lot of the work, complete all the repairs to the ceilings, walls, and floors first, then move on to prepping and painting the walls. While the walls are drying, you can tackle any building projects (such as making shelves or a bed) you have planned. Try to do as much as you can in as short a time as possible. There's nothing worse than living with a makeover project in process, but you can get a lot done in a weekend if you power through. Crank up the tunes— music is a great motivator—crank up the tools, and crank up the whole enterprise a notch.

Finding Your Own Style

What does it mean when someone's home has "great style"? To me it doesn't mean that the home is stylish in the trendy sense of the word. Rather, I think of great style as design cohesiveness that's appealing to the eye and, most important, reflective of who lives in the home. **Your home shouldn't just have style; it should have *your* style**. All the little things that make you different from other people should be apparent in the design of your home. When it comes to style, stay true to yourself.

So what is your style? There is something about you that stands out, whether it's how you dress, the way you talk, the way you act, or what and who you love: all the things that make you *you*. Some people wear their style on their sleeves; others have a subtler approach. Still others are like an onion—you have to peel back the layers to find out what's underneath to get a fix on their style.

When we go into a home on *EMHE*, we have a very brief time to get some clues to a family's style. But little things can tell us a lot. What books do they read? What type of music do they listen to? (If there's a lot of Grateful Dead, it's always safe to work some tie-dye in there somewhere.) Do they collect anything? What kind of clothes and accessories do they wear? That's a big one. Probably the biggest clue to your own sense of style is hanging in your closet right now. In fact, the bedroom on pages 68–69 was based entirely on a very graphic black-and-white purse that I saw in the house we were about to make over. "Is that your bag?" I asked the mom whose bedroom, shared with her husband (and a retreat from their sextuplets), was my secret project for the show. "Yes," she replied. "It's my favorite. I love the design." That purse ultimately served as inspiration for the finished room: an almost entirely black-and-white space, every bit as elegant and graphic as the mom's bag.

If you're having trouble figuring out where to begin, it might help to settle on a general interior design style like Victorian, Country French, mid-century modern, Southwestern, Asian, or an arts and crafts look. Your choice can guide your selection of furniture, paint colors, and room accessories. No matter what, though, keep an open mind and don't feel as though everything you put in your home has to match one particular style.

Still, it's good to have a jumping-off point. I created the following quiz to help you determine the direction that's right for you. It's possible that you're already one-hundred percent sure about what you want. In that case, take the quiz anyway, just for fun.

If, however, you tend to buy only things you like, then go home and find that they don't work in the grand scheme of things, the questions I provide might help you focus your efforts. And who knows, maybe there is an inner you that has never really been properly expressed in your home.

Before you take the quiz, let me say this about having a "style": You may like ethnic design or industrial modern or retro '70s style, but what you want to do is take that look and make it your own. That's what's really going to make your place look and feel great. So sharpen your pencil, answer the following questions, and read on to learn more about how to use your natural design inclinations to successfully make over your home.

What's Your Style?

1. The places you like to shop include:

a. uncluttered contemporary stores where white, black, and a little gunmetal gray reign.

b. flea markets, garage sales, thrift shops.

c. department and specialty stores with wide-ranging choices; quality antique stores.

d. stores that showcase the handcrafted wares of other cultures.

e. shops with environmentally responsible items made from natural materials.

f. all of the above.

2. The museum show you'd run to see is:

a. twenty cutting-edge London artists under twenty.

b. French advertising posters from the '20s.

c. Rembrandt and the Dutch Masters.

d. Tibetan treasures.

e. an Ansel Adams retrospective.

f. all of the above.

3. Your clothes tend to be:

a. white or black.

b. funky—vintage pieces mixed with new.

c. buttoned-down and conservative with lots of khaki.

d. African-print shirts or Indian skirts.

e. jeans, organic cotton T-shirts, and boots.

f. all of the above.

4. The music you favor is:

a. intellectual rock like Radiohead, the White Stripes.

b. pop like John Mayer and Sheryl Crow.

c. classics like old Sinatra and new Diana Krall.

d. world music like the Gipsy Kings and Buena Vista Social Club.

e. earthy and raw-edged like Bob Dylan and Johnny Cash.

f. all of the above.

5. Your favorite movies from another era are:

a. mod films from the '60s like *Blow-Up* and *Bullitt*.

b. *Casablanca* and film noir flicks like *The Maltese Falcon*.

c. anything with Cary Grant or Audrey Hepburn.

d. *Out of Africa* and foreign films like the Brazilian *Black Orpheus*.

e. *Born Free* and nature documentaries.

f. all of the above.

6. Your idea of a great vacation spot is:

a. Stockholm.

b. Paris.

c. a golf resort in Hawaii.

d. the farthest reaches of Mexico.

e. the mountains of Wyoming.

f. all of the above.

7. Your favorite type of restaurant is:

a. the "it" spot everyone is talking about.

b. funky old Italian dives with checked table-cloths and red leather banquettes.

c. the classic steak house.

d. Ethiopian restaurants and ethnic food hole-in-the-walls.

e. organic eateries.

f. all of the above.

8. You like to throw parties that are:

a. evening soirées with chic cocktails and gourmet hors d'oeuvres.

b. casual buffets that let you break out all your flea market bowls.

c. sit-down dinners served on your grand-mother's china.

d. Indian or Catalonian food nights.

e. barbecues on the beach over an open campfire.

f. all of the above.

If you answered mostly **a**, your style is minimalist.

I'm going to go out on a limb here and say that you probably don't have lace curtains in your dining room, fringe on your pillows, or Grranimals in your closet. Chances are, you like a home that's clean and modern and maybe you even stick to a palette of all white: white napkins, white towels, white sheets, white walls, white shirts. Maybe you even eat white cheeses and have a white dog. (You still, though, cling to your black leather jacket; that you'll never give up.) You might also like vintage modern but only as long as it fits in with your minimalist scheme. You're undoubtedly up on the latest in art, music, and design. You're hip, you're mod, you know what's going on.

I'm an admirer of modern minimalism (not to mention the latest hip things). Keep in mind, though, that your home is more than a showcase for what's new and cutting-edge; it's also a place where you and your family and friends should be able to feel comfortable and relaxed. If everything is flawless, you may be miserable. I respect the fact that you always have a coaster handy for the person who wants to put a drink down on your one-of-a-kind industrial coffee table, but don't be afraid to let your guard down a little. You need at least a few pieces of furniture that aren't works of art but places to curl up or put your feet on after a long day.

You want to live in a home not a museum. Sit on your couch and wrap yourself up in that lumpy blanket your mother crocheted, maybe even put on the ugly plaid pajamas that Uncle Jerry bought you, and survey the landscape. Think about how you can make your home both a temple of minimalism and an inviting, restful place. You might try mixing in a few organic elements like plants or natural wood pieces, as well as a little color. Think about furnishing your home not only with what's hot, but also with what gives you a warm feeling. Make it personal and you're on your way to creating a home that, while still chic, is a place where people want to hang out.

If you answered mostly **b**, your style is maximalist.

Okay, it's not really a word—I made it up—but I think it describes perfectly the kind of person who just can't get enough of, well, stuff. Your idea of heaven is probably Queen's Day in the Netherlands, a day when everyone breaks out all their old things and sells them in the street. In Amsterdam, it's basically one big citywide flea market. Going into your house is like going into a high-end garage sale, and you've got collections galore: lamps, movie posters, pottery, old radios, silver spoons. When you walk into a thrift store, you get an adrenaline rush (and just a little high from sniffing the mothballs).

You probably like to stay home and nest with all your finds, but you're also a pretty fun and enthusiastic person to be around. And if it sounds like I know you all too well, it's because I do: I, too, collect vintage wares. I've got *a lot* of stuff . . . but I also try hard to rein it in so that my house doesn't feel like it's bursting at the seams. After all, sometimes "collector" is just a polite term for "pack rat." So try to open up your home and give yourself more space. Pick the best of your old radios and arts and craft pottery; leave some empty wall space between retro posters. From experience, I can tell you that you'll feel so much better about your place if you can actually *see* what you have. Concentrate your design efforts on creating rooms that are airy and well edited when it comes to showing off your finds.

If you answered mostly **c**, your style is traditionalist.

They just don't make things like they used to—that thought probably pops into your mind pretty often.

For that reason, you tend to keep things the same. I'm willing to bet that you've got lots of family heirlooms in your home and those pieces that haven't been handed down look like they could have been. You're probably most comfortable with elements of style that are nice but not showy. Elements like a sofa covered in a subtle paisley fabric, a quality Oriental rug, or maybe a maple four-poster bed with a white chenille spread.

There's nothing wrong with being a traditionalist, and I'm with you on the fact that sometimes there's nothing better than a classic. We *should* hang on to some things that have been around forever (like letter writing—I bet you still send letters through the mail). That said, does it have to be steak and potatoes every night? If you keep your home too traditional, you risk it feeling boring and stale after awhile. So consider spicing it up a bit. Maybe paint one wall in your house an offbeat tangerine and trade in your Oriental for a chunky sisal rug. Perhaps you could replace your chenille bedspread with an Indian print or some modern color-blocked bedding. Obviously, you'll need to use a careful eye to blend the traditional with splashes of nontraditional, but that's the only way to make your home seem like yours—not your parents' or your grandparents'. Loosen up a little and look beyond the familiar to find a style that's truly your own.

If you answered mostly d, your style is ethnologist.

Although this sounds like you administer anesthesia, what it means is that you're into different cultures: ethnology is the comparison of cultures (so glad I have a dictionary on my computer). In other words, you like things kind of worldly. You probably love to travel (or at least take armchair journeys through the Travel Channel) to out-of-the-way places where life is extremely different from your own. And your clothing probably reflects it. Maybe you've got lots of cool jewelry from around the world, and you dig anything that's handcrafted and representative of the art of an indigenous culture. I wouldn't be surprised if you've got tapestries and African masks on the wall, Balinese furniture, rugs from the Middle East, and Chinese cooking utensils. Maybe there's even Indian incense burning and beads hanging in your doorway (which reminds me of my mom's ethnic phase in the '70s, although I think the incense might have been more a necessity owing to our very bowel-troubled dogs than a nod to India).

One highlight of my own travels is to bring home beautiful things made by other cultures, so I see the appeal of ethnic chic. Where you can get into trouble, as with anything else, is by overdoing it. I personally love to see ethnic pieces mixed in with complementary modern pieces from our own culture (see page 62 for a good example of that). Again, you want to make your home a reflection of your personality so, while you may have a deep feeling for another culture— maybe that culture is even part of your ancestry—do try to mix in elements of your own life. For instance, one family I know has antique Japanese dressers and a few Japanese prints in their bedroom combined with a soft rug (rather than, say, tatami mats) and contemporary American bedding. When you walk into their room you don't feel like you've been transported to Tokyo, but instead get a nice taste of Japan and a big bite of their own personal style.

If you answered mostly e, your style is naturalist.

If you're a naturalist, you probably not only love anything having to do with nature, you're very protective of the natural world. Maybe your home is filled with items made from recycled materials; you might even have solar energy. Perhaps you're vegan. I'm guessing that you have plants around the house, lots of nice wood furniture (including a coffee table laden with *National Geographic* and *Outside* magazines), and that the predominant shades in your home are earth tones. You might have some souvenirs from your trips to the beach, mountains, and desert lying around: shells, pinecones, rocks. On the walls are landscape photos and maybe even a shot or two of polar bears.

To tell the truth, I'm stoked that you're a naturalist. I'm all for bringing the outdoors in and for using renewable resources like bamboo flooring. But of course, I've also got a few caveats about the potential for naturalism to turn ugly. First, be aware that when you bring Mother Nature into your home—whether it's driftwood, shells, starfish, leaves and branches, or anything else right off the land or sand—it may bring along some little friends, namely bugs that will end up all over your sheets. Before you bring some of those things home they need to be kiln dried, treated, and sealed to make sure they're house-ready. So don't be just a naturalist, be a realist.

The other thing is, go easy on the earth tones. Even though it's nice to do your home in warm beiges and browns, don't forget that nature is also a source of incredibly vibrant, gorgeous color. Think of the oranges of autumn, the new green of spring, the turquoise of the Mediterranean, the purple mountains' majesty. Bringing in some color doesn't compromise your devotion to what's natural; it just gives it more life and greater depth. If you can do that—as well as quit terrorizing your friends who don't recycle and refrain from bringing home every stray dog in the city—you're going to have a great house and a pretty nice life.

If you answered mostly f, your style is all of the above. That is, you're me.

That's right, I am a minimalist, maximalist, traditionalist, ethnologist, and naturalist all rolled up into one. For instance, I love modern furniture and clean lines.

There are areas in my home that are very simple and actually kind of spare. But that's only one facet of me. I am also a collector. I collect vintage guitars, vintage furniture, and vintage fabrics among other things. I do try to organize them well and periodically reduce the number I have, but, you maximalists who have to cope with chaos? I feel your pain.

While I probably fall less into the traditionalist area than any of the other categories, I do have certain traditions that I can't seem to break. I wear the same pair of jeans every day (well, not the same actual pair, but the same style), and I have worn my corduroy jacket for so long it probably belongs in a museum. My choices aren't necessarily conservative, but if I find something I'm crazy about, I cling to it. That's why you'll find me eating in the same Thai restaurant three times a week, chowing down on green curry even as my dining companions are complaining that it's getting a little mundane.

Then there's the ethnologist side of me. You name it—Japanese sandals, lithographs, and kimono fabrics; Costa Rican and Indian textiles; Mexican tiles; Spanish wines; African beads; Native American artifacts and blankets; Eskimo artwork—I've got it. Part of the fun of traveling is finding these little gems and bringing them home as reminders of my trips.

And as if that's not enough, I want to incorporate nature into my home as well. Greenery, some earth tones, bamboo. Yep, that's all there, and I'm all for going green in the save-the-planet-sense, too.

Okay, so how does this all work? First, let's give it its proper name: eclectic. If you're like me and love many styles, designing your home can be challenging. But putting your eclectic taste to work can also be a lot of fun. What it mainly takes is being judicious and finding some continuity among all those disparate objects and styles. When you do that, the result can be great. You wind up surrounded by all the things you love and living in a home that reflects all the different sides of you. On pages 138–43 you'll see how I managed to pull it all together in my living and entertaining room.

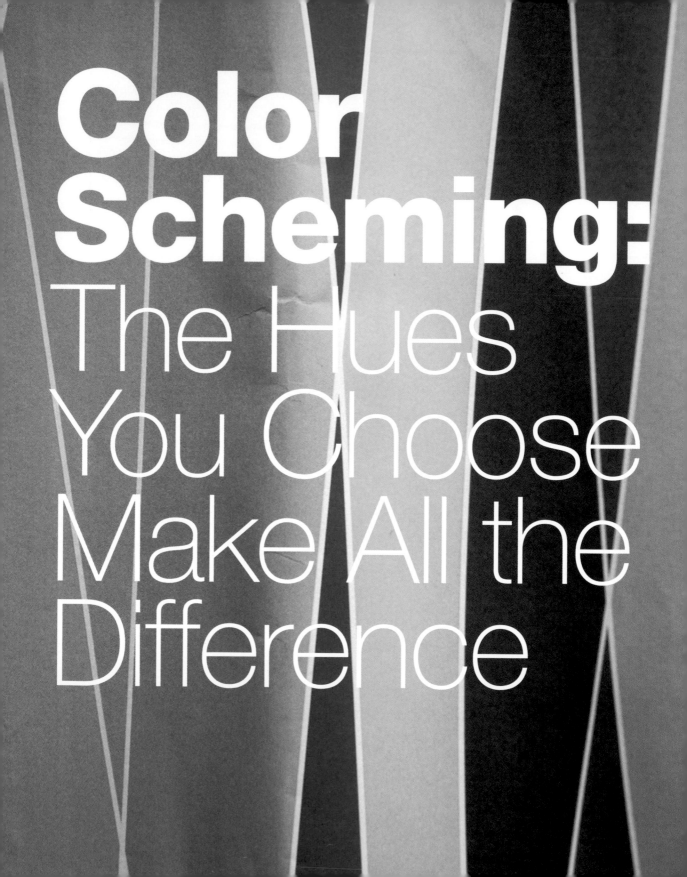

Color Scheming: The Hues You Choose Make All the Difference

What's your favorite color? I know, it sounds like a bad pick-up line someone might throw at you at a bar, but considering that you're not in a bar (are you?) and that you're contemplating how to redo a room, I think it's an appropriate question. And now that you've answered it, forget about it. Not that it isn't perfectly fine to bring in your favorite color or colors when you're making over a space, but what's most important to think about is how **the colors you choose affect the mood of the room you're designing**, how well they go together, and how they figure into giving the room some visual impact.

Color is the first thing that hits you when you walk into a room, and it can immediately change how you feel. So yes, of course, choose colors you like, but also choose colors that are going to evoke the ambiance you're going for. While turquoise might be your favorite color, is it really the shade you want to look at on a dining room wall while you're trying to eat? (Maybe if you're trying to lose weight. The blues are considered so unappetizing that diet book writers sometimes recommend blue as an appetite suppressant.) Seriously, it's great if you're partial to red, but walls the color of a sports car might be too stimulating for a bedroom you hope to turn into a space for relaxation and quiet reflection.

So think about the mood you're going for, then consider two other factors: harmony and "pop" or, as it's sometimes called, accent. Harmony is achieved when the colors you put on your walls work well with the colors you've planned for everything else in the room, including the floors, windows, furniture, bedding, and even the artwork. Pop refers to the color or colors in a room (though it could be a texture, too) that stand out. Pop gives your eye somewhere to go. Without it, the room and everything in it blend together and you won't really see any of it. A room without pop may be one where everything is flat, neutral, and just, well, bland. Everything literally fades into the woodwork. Or it may be a room with too many competing colors so that nothing is particularly noticeable—or notable. To my mind, pop is an integral element of style. It even sounds exciting. *Pop!!*

Sometime in your life, elementary school perhaps, you probably learned the basic principles of color. What's warm, what's cool, primary, secondary, and so on. All that can be helpful, but I think the process of choosing colors for your home can be simpler if you use your instincts and concentrate on the three factors I just mentioned: mood, harmony, and pop. To give you a better sense of what I mean, let's take them one at a time.

Mood

You're probably naturally drawn to certain colors and, whether you intend them to or not, those colors say a lot about you. If you're wearing yellow all the time, you're probably a very happy, perky person. Maybe you even annoy people, you're so happy. If you show up in black every day (and don't live in New York City, where wearing black all the time means only that you live in New York City), you're probably pretty sober and serious, maybe even a touch intellectual. Lavender? You're going to be pegged as romantic and sexy. Red? Extroverted, you're on fire. If none of those judgments is surprising it's because we all make associations with color. What most people are less overtly aware of is that color can transform how you feel. If you weren't exactly cheery before you put on that orange shirt, you probably are now. Sit in a room that's all shades of pale cream and off-white and you can't help but go a little Zen.

In some ways, the easiest way to make over a room is to just fill it with things that you like. But I highly

recommend thinking more strategically so that you not only surround yourself with colors and things you appreciate, but give the room an aura. Let it have a purpose beyond the obvious. Make it not just for sleeping, for working, for watching TV, but for de-stressing, for daydreaming, for finding inspiration. And the best way to do that is to choose paint colors with intent. A perfect example is the room I did on pages 50–53. Ordinarily I prefer bedroom colors to be mellow so that the room feels relaxing or romantic. But in this case I wanted to bring in lively, happy shades to inject some joy into the life of the woman I was designing the room for. The greens, reds, and oranges I used stood for the fresh beginning I was hoping she would have.

Colors can impart elation, serenity, humor—almost anything. They can also give you a sensation of coolness when the weather is hot, and help you warm up when the weather is cool. Paint your walls aqua blue, minty green, or icy white and you'll likely feel refreshed every time you walk in the door—just

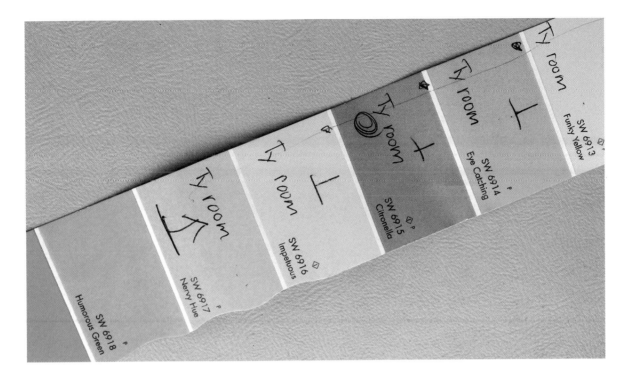

what you want if you're living somewhere steamy like the Florida Keys. Using mocha, cinnamon, or persimmon, on the other hand, can make a room feel cozy, the perfect cocoon if you live in a place like Minnesota where it drops below zero.

But while each color has what you might call a certain temperature and personality, you can soften it by toning down the hue's depth, brightness, or saturation. Green, for instance, makes you think of nature and is a good color to use when you want to bring the outdoors in. Yet painting a wall forest green is a lot more audacious than painting one a delicate celadon green. Likewise, both carnation pink and pearl pink give a room a feminine look, but the carnation pink is younger, more flirtatious than the subtler and more sophisticated pearl pink. Think of it like volume control. The basic hues set the mood; their darkness, lightness, and depth determine how profoundly you feel them. You might like loud music, but could you live in a loud room?

One last thing about using color to convey a mood: You don't have to paint the whole room one color just to get your point across (and more often than not, you probably shouldn't). Sometimes you'll want the ceiling to be a different color, particularly if it's low— using a light shade will make it appear higher. Other times you may want to do what I often do, which is to use your "mood" color on a single "accent wall." That's the wall that I want to be the focal point of the room and painting it a different color makes it pop—which I'll talk about more in a minute.

Harmony

How important is it that colors "match"? Well, there's matching and then there's *matching*. You might see a lady who's dressed top to bottom in mocha, then notice that her Chihuahua is the same color. When you go to her house it turns out all the walls and the furniture are brown, light brown, and maybe light, light brown. Some people just like to match completely—their clothes, their animals, their

sofa, everything. And that's what I'd call matching too much. (Or, in Ms. Brown's case, I'd call it a cry for help.)

In fact, colors don't necessarily need to match, but they need to harmonize so they don't fight each other for attention. And which colors harmonize is not set in stone. You've really got to put colors together and use your eye to see what works. If this is intimidating—let's just say you've already been told that color isn't your strong point (Was it so wrong to wear an orange striped top and purple check skirt to your sister's wedding?) then look around you to see what color choices other people have made. You can start with your style folder: Look at all those pictures you tore out of magazines. Next go to your closet and look at clothes you own that have patterns or plaids. What colors did the designers team together? Check out gardens, stationery, labels on foods at the grocery store. There are hundreds of examples of color harmony all around you.

You're less likely to go wrong if you try and keep the number of colors you have in a room to three, four at the most, with one or two of those colors being neutral. I'm not saying that more colors can't work, but keeping it to a minimum makes it more likely that you can find colors that complement one another. And I'm not just talking about paint and furniture colors. I'm talking about everything you put in a room, from window shades and bedding to rugs and big pieces of artwork.

There are a couple of other things you can also do to find colors that harmonize well. First, experiment with the shades you like right on your walls. Don't just hold up little swatch cards and extrapolate in your mind. Paint fairly big circles or squares of color next to each other so that you can see how they really look together. This will also give you a chance to see if the colors look different in your home than they do in the can. Colors take on a different cast depending on where they are. The location of your windows, what kind of lighting you own, what part of the country you live in, and what's directly outside your door reflecting in, are all going to affect how your walls look so check them out both when the sun is streaming in and at night when the lights are on. Then give it three days before you make a decision.

And by the way, while you're looking at how well the colors play on your wall, also think about whether they harmonize with the other rooms in your home. You don't need to paint all your rooms one color or even stick to colors in the same tonal range. It is nice, though, if all those rooms have some common thread. It might be that the intensity of the different shades are on par, or that they all share a certain quality. In my old house in Atlanta, for instance, the lower halves of the walls in the kitchen were painted a cantaloupe-y orange, the living room had a couple of walls painted mustard, and the bedroom was painted all in avocado. Besides providing evidence that I always have food on my mind, all the colors had a yellow base and were fairly earthy. Yep, I like to eat and I like nature, too.

Pop

You're going to read a lot about "pop" in this book, because I think it's a critical element of design, and I always use it in some way to liven up the rooms I make over. There are a lot of ways to use color to create pop. You can go for the accent wall that I mentioned earlier: Paint one wall a deeper, brighter, or more intense color than the other walls in the room. Or cover it with wallpaper, which is a great way to add pop, too. You can keep all the walls neutral—painted, say, ivory, taupe, or a pale, pale beige—and bring in furniture that pops, perhaps some vintage leather armchairs in silvery blue or a buttery yellow sofa. In an office, it might be bookshelves painted a surprising shade of red that punches up the room.

Neutrals in particular provide a great backdrop for pop. Just like the matte surrounding a picture in a frame, neutrals make what you want to draw attention to come into focus. But keeping the walls toned down and using the furniture for contrast isn't the only way to create pop in a neutral room. If

you like the idea of a fairly monochromatic scheme (e.g., dark blue, blue, and light blue), you can also choose furniture in neutral tones, then add different textures to bring in pop. A bumpy jute rug; a sofa slip covered in a raw, natural linen; a bedspread with a chunky weave—playing off the smoothness of plastered walls and wood floors, these all give the eye something to gravitate toward, even if they too are in subdued shades.

Another way to inject a bit of pop into a neutral room is with accessories like colored glass bottles or vases filled with vividly-hued flowers; curtains in a striking pattern; or a hanging lamp that throws an unexpected burst of color into the room. Neutrals also let you use beautiful wood furniture for pop. When there are few color distractions, you can see the fine grain of a teak credenza, the variations of tone in a cherry table, and carvings in a mahogany headboard.

One thing to remember about pop is that it doesn't have to be what you traditionally think of as a color that "pops." A white bed against an aqua wall is going to pop; so will a black one. Black-and-white photos hung on a China red backdrop are going to pop. And it doesn't have to be a particularly bright color either. In my home, I covered my fireplace with a mix of muted blue, green, and orangish tiles. The wall behind them is a shade of mocha light enough to avoid competing with the tiles and make the fireplace a focal point of the room. Pop doesn't have to be loud; it just has to offer enough contrast to stand out. *Snap!*

What you're going for here is drama, a little or a lot, depending on your overall concept for the room. But even if you're going for high drama, be careful about overdoing it. What you *don't* want to do is flood the room with all kinds of colors that compete for attention. You want a room that has punch, not a room that looks punch drunk.

Show Your True Colors

You can fade a color back, crank up its volume, give it shimmer, make it dimmer, but it's still going to retain the essence of its original self. What is that essence and what will it say about the room you feature it in? What do the colors you love say about you? Here's my take on the basic six.

red

The mood it sets: Dramatic, energetic

Who loves it: If you're into red, you're probably a really dynamic, confident person. Red speaks loudly. If you want to paint your bedroom a bold red, chances are you're a pretty bold person.

blue

The mood it sets: Calm, cool, collected

Who loves it: Blue, the color of the ocean and the sky, evokes tranquility, so if you're into blue, you're probably pretty relaxed, kind of chill. You like the simple things in life.

yellow

The mood it sets: Joyous, warm

Who loves it: Yellow is the happiest color out there, so if you're drawn to it, you probably have a pretty sunny disposition. You're a lot of fun to be around. You're perky, you think the glass is half full, and you want to share your awesome vibes with everyone.

green

The mood it sets: Balanced, restful

Who loves it: Green lovers are usually tree huggers; that is, they're outdoorsy and into the environment. If green is your favorite color, you're probably very down to earth.

orange

The mood it sets: Cheery, fun

Who loves it: Orange is a color for people who are creative and willing to go out on a limb a bit. You're probably lively, love a good party, and have a fairly optimistic nature.

purple

The mood it sets: Passionate, sexy, romantic

Who loves it: People with an affinity for purple tend to be seductive and mysterious. Purple is also the color of the counterculture, so if this is your color you're probably a little rebellious, too. I bet you have a tattoo.

Inspiration

When most people begin a makeover project, their inclination is to think about styles and colors they like as well as practical needs, like more storage. All good, but I urge you to also **go a little deeper and look for something that you find either meaningful or beautiful** and let it inspire your design. On *Extreme Makeover,* we send the families on vacation while we redo their homes, but before they go, I try to get a real sense of what's important to them, whether it's a philanthropic cause, their original homeland, nature, objects that they collect, places they love, or even the memories of a particular person. Every room you'll see in this book was designed, not arbitrarily but with something about the people who live in it in mind. Whatever inspires them in life became the inspiration for my design.

also get inspiration in a larger sense from the impact our work has on the people we help, especially the kids. Any time I'm feeling worn out from being on the road so much, I've only to reread the thank-you letter I received from twelve-year-old Abigail Gilliam (and, believe me, I've read it many, many times!) and I get an energy surge. You can see the letter on the opposite page. Abigail's father died suddenly, leaving a wife and six young kids. From the autopsy report the family discovered that the house they were living in was full of toxic spores. Abigail's gratitude for the safe, clean house we ultimately built for the family reminds me why I have the best job in the world.

Another source of inspiration for me is a copy of the lyrics to a song written by Siehera Thibodeau, a very ill twelve-year-old (check out her room on pages 130–132). While in the hospital after heart surgery (one of many), Siehera wrote a song asking God to let her parents know how much she loves them and doesn't want them to worry. Every time I read the lyrics and think about Siehera, it just tears me apart that she has had to go through so much at her young age. But it also keeps me positive and doing what I'm doing because I know that, when you're twelve years old and coming home after a long medical ordeal, it's nice to have a beautiful, comfortable place to live. More than nice. It's what everyone deserves.

What inspires the design of your own home can be any number of things. Your inspiration can come from something incredibly meaningful to you—your children or your Italian ancestry—or it could come

August 13, 2006

Dear Ty,

I can't thank you enough for all that you have done! You really are the best!!! You do so much good things for familys like us, you and your design team give familys a new start in life. Monday morning I was very nervous about the whole thing with all the cameras and meeting the design team, but once I met you I felt like I knew you all my life. Your just regular people like me. Ty, I really don't know how I could thank you enough for all you have done for our family. This is the greatest thing anyone could ever give. This is my dads dream come true. He always wanted to meet you. Thank you so much for saving the memorial, that means so much to me. Thank you so much I have been thinking of you guys this whole vacation! We have had such a fun time going out to eat with Andy. I really hope we can see all of you sometime soon. I can't wait to say "Bus driver move that bus". Thank you so so much Ty. Sincerely

Abigail Gilliam

from something you simply find appealing. Maybe you rescue animals. Maybe you really love horses and the look associated with them (such as horse blankets, rustic stables, and saddle leather). Maybe your inspiration is a beach house in the Outer Banks or an exquisite hotel you stayed at in London or Paris. Maybe it's some great photographs of your family, a collection of arts and crafts pottery, or your love of music. Your inspiration could even be a poster, as it was with a dance studio I designed for a woman in Virginia.

This woman, Carol Crawford-Smith, had been a star member of the Dance Theatre of Harlem ensemble and later became a dance teacher. She developed multiple sclerosis and lost control of her body, the tool with which she had expressed herself so beautifully. My inspiration for the studio was an old poster of her from her days as a member of the ballet company. It wasn't so much that I wanted to replicate the look of the poster, but I wanted to replicate the mood that it evoked. My mom, who used to be a dancer herself, found the quote "To dance is divine—it lifts the spirit in all of us" which I painted on the wall.

To create a bedroom for a couple proud of its South Pacific heritage, I hung grass cloth wallpaper on the walls and used bedding I designed called Bali Hai. I also took photographs of watercolor paintings on old Hawaiian menus, blew them up, and made artwork out of them. I wanted the couple to feel as though they were back in Polynesia.

If you don't yet have any particular inspiration for the room you want to make over, think about your hobbies, your heritage, your role models, and your passions. Let them be your guides. Another place to look is the world around you. Inspiration is everywhere. A friend's shirt may catch your eye and help you discover a great combination of colors for your walls. Catch a glimpse of a leather belt next to a crisp white shirt and a lightbulb may go off: Wow, leather chairs would look great against a simple white wall. The cool gray of stones on a beach; the color of sand against a turquoise sea; the vibrant, multicolored fabrics of India; flowers in a garden—these can all be jumping-off points for your design.

I've found inspiration in many unlikely places. I once took photographs of an old, scuffed-up tile floor in a restaurant—it had no discernible pattern but a mix of great shades of blue—and translated it into a design for bedding (you can see it on page 105). It's pretty crazy to think a filthy tile floor ended up being the muse for something you can wrap yourself up in, but that's how inspiration works. You just have to open your eyes and your mind.

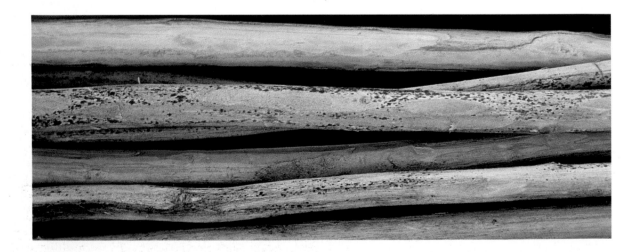

Part II
Sleeping Spaces

Probably because it's the least public room in the house, the bedroom is usually the last room people put on their to-do list. Or maybe it's because they're thinking, "I'm going to be asleep anyway, what does it matter what my room looks like?" Well, that's kind of the point. If your bedroom were a place that was great to hang out in, you might use it for more than sleeping. And when you *are* asleep, you might even have a more restful night if the room were set up comfortably. This, after all, is the room that you dream in, so dream big.

What is it that you've always wanted in a bedroom? Whether it's an antique four-poster bed with fabric draped around the top, or a rough-hewn headboard and furnishings with a Western feel, or a room that's sleek, chic, and modern, you owe it to yourself to see your vision through.

And if you don't have a vision yet, I hope the bedrooms on the following pages will inspire you. I think you'll see that there are many different ways to go, depending on your personal style and how much of a makeover you're willing or able to tackle. If you have the time and resources to do a complete overhaul, definitely go for it, but keep in mind that tweaking one or two elements in the room can also have a big impact. Maybe it's just a matter of changing the art or the bedding; maybe you need only paint the walls and do some careful editing. It doesn't matter what you choose to do, as long as you're true to yourself. In the end, the bedroom that tells a story about who you are and what you love is going to be the bedroom where you have your sweetest dreams.

Sudden
Impact

In most homes, bedrooms tend to be on the quiet side, with the "wow factor" left to more public spaces like living and dining rooms. But **there's no law that says a bedroom can't also be high impact** (and if there is, well, rules are meant to be broken). In fact, sometimes bright, mood-elevating splashes of color are just what the doctor ordered. There is, though, a smart way to go about creating a bedroom that's fun and lighthearted. After all, you don't want to turn up the volume so high that it's impossible to sleep.

ABOVE Photographs of flowers were enlarged, printed out on canvas, and stretched over frames to make inexpensive artwork.

OPPOSITE PAGE Fun, attention-getting bursts of color work in a bedroom if they're balanced with muted tones and clean-lined accessories. The extras are kept to a minimum with only a few understated lamps and a couple of elegant floor vases. Likewise, when your headboard is ornate, keep the bedding simple. Here, all we needed for oomph was a few flowered throw pillows.

A balance between high spirits and livability is what I was going for when I created a bedroom for a woman by the name of Colleen Nick. One summer night, Colleen and her eldest daughter, Morgan, traveled to a nearby Arkansas town to watch a Little League baseball game. During the game, six-year-old Morgan joined her friends to catch fireflies in an adjacent field and was never seen again. She simply disappeared, possibly abducted by a man who witnesses saw watching her. That was in 1995, but Colleen has never given up hope that she will one day be reunited with her eldest daughter (she also has two other children, a boy and girl). After her loss, she established the Morgan Nick Foundation and she's worked tirelessly ever since to help other families find lost children and to implement protective measures so that kids don't get abducted in the first place. Colleen is an absolutely incredible woman.

After years of neglect while the family concentrated on finding Morgan, the Nick house was in a pretty sorry state. The carpet had gotten so bad that they had ripped it out and were padding around on bare concrete floors. (Her son and his friends, though, thought it was cool—they were skateboarding on them.)

While the *EMHE* crew worked on giving the Nick family a new house, I joined in on some of the continuing efforts to find Morgan. I was helping to put a time-enhanced photograph of what Morgan might look like now on a billboard next to a highway when I looked down and there, growing out of a cinderblock amidst old tires and machine parts, was one little yellow daisy. This one small flower, somehow surviving in the middle of all this junk and trash, seemed like the perfect metaphor for Colleen herself. With all the pain and suffering she endures, I thought she deserved a room that brought some light and joy into her life. And that daisy, unabashedly bold and bright, was the perfect inspiration.

But while I wanted Colleen's bedroom to exude exuberance, I also wanted it to be a place where

she could relax—a little hard to do if the walls are screaming at you. So here was the compromise: I saved the bright bursts of color for the artwork I created to adorn the room, then painted the walls a deep, but fairly muted mustard yellow and light olive green. Because they're associated with nature, both shades symbolize new growth, but neither was going to keep Colleen up at night.

To create the flower pictures above the dressers and on either side of the bed, I took digital photographs of daisies and sunflowers and transferred them to my computer. I then enlarged the flowers and deepened their red and orange hues so that, once framed (they're printed on canvas), they'd really pop off the yellow and green walls. I also carried the flower motif over to the solid maple bedroom set I custom built for Colleen. The wood is unstained, a good choice when you want to keep the look light.

The real key to making any room with strong visual elements work is restraint. In Colleen's bedroom that meant letting the flower photos and the carved bedroom set be the main attractions by keeping everything else in the room simple. There are, for instance, no rugs on the floor and, save for a few flowered throw pillows, no other patterns in the room. The bedding—including the fabric encircling the head of the bed—is solid so that it doesn't compete with the other patterns in the room and lets the pure joy of those flowers shine through.

To this day, Colleen sends me emails telling me how much she loves the room. She's finally accepted the idea that she can take a moment to enjoy herself without having to feel guilty.

While I kept patterns to a minimum in Colleen's room, I'm all for mixing them when the time is right.

The room I did for breast cancer survivor Shawna Farina is the perfect example of a wild mix that works. Combining different patterns is always tricky, and sometimes you just have to rely on your eye. What makes for harmony in this particular instance is that the patterns are of varying size and in the same colors. Mixed motifs don't always have to be in the

ABOVE A piece of glass fitted over the bedside table protects the wood from sloshing cups of coffee and other possible stain perpetrators.

OPPOSITE PAGE Pictures can have as much impact propped as hung.

FOLLOWING SPREAD One reason the mix of patterns in this room works is that the patterns are of varying sizes. Another distinctive feature of this room is the use of pendant fixtures on either side of the bed instead of table lamps.

same shades (though they usually work best if they share one or two colors), but it is a good idea to team up patterns of different sizes. If all the patterns are big, you could be in for a big crazy mess; if all the patterns are small, you risk the room looking fussy and overdone.

The reason I chose to create such a bold room for Shawna and her husband is because Shawna herself is so bold and strong. When her mom was twenty-nine, she was diagnosed with breast cancer, so Shawna grew up knowing all about this dreadful disease. But her mom survived and Shawna was so inspired that she created a walk/run called Relay for Life to raise money and awareness for cancer research. Although the fundraiser only takes place in the small Indiana town where Shawna lives, she has raised close to half a million dollars in five years.

One year when she was getting dressed for the relay she found a lump in her own breast. At twenty-six with three young kids it seemed insane that something like this could happen. She had to go through chemotherapy, radiation, a mastectomy, and hysterectomy, all the while still participating in Relay for Life and working part time, not to mention

leading her daughters' Brownie troop! But like her mom, Shawna beat back the cancer.

By the time we showed up, Shawna's family was in pretty dire financial straits; all their money had gone toward hospital bills. They barely even had any furniture. But—and this is just one measure of Shawna's can-do spirit—she took old Christmas wrapping paper and framed it so that her kids would have something bright and colorful on the walls to look at. I loved that idea so much that I used it to inspire the room's accent wall and bedding, both of which have wrapping paper–esque patterns.

Red is a dynamic color not everyone would want to live with it, but for Shawna it was a good fit. She and her husband are young and very hip, so I kept the look modern with a steel-framed bed, globe lights, and a buttery leather Eames chair. Yet it's not stark modern; the chrysanthemum mural and "flocked" bedding give the room a sense of humor. To me, though, the room's crowning glory is the wrapping paper art above the Eames chair. It's a reminder of Shawna's ingenuity, appreciation for beauty, and fortitude.

LEFT: To give the headboard wall an iridescent glow, I cut square panels, painted them the same red and white pattern, mounted them about six inches from the wall, and placed little lights behind them.

OPPOSITE PAGE: Taking my cue from Shawna, I wrapped paper around boards and hung them as art. When she walked into the room and realized I'd referenced her own decorating ideas, it put a huge smile on her face. That's when I know that I've done my job.

Inspired by Art

I'm not among those people who think you should buy art to match the furniture. I'm the kind of guy who buys art from the heart, then worries about how it's going to look in my house later. But that said, **if you already own art that you love, why not design the room to showcase it** or at least let it be your inspiration? The driving force behind the design of a room for a woman named Veronica Ginyard was her collection of carved masks, gifts she'd received from friends and family who'd traveled to Africa.

eronica is a lovely and incredibly strong woman, who extricated herself from domestic abuse and is single-handedly raising her eight children (including two sets of twins). At the time we entered the picture, the family was living in a small house with exposed live wires sticking out of the wall and mold from the constant flooding of their basement. The place was really a wreck, and the kids were all crammed together in attic and basement rooms that were dangerous and stifling.

While my goal was to display Veronica's collection of masks to good effect, I also wanted to create a restful environment for this woman who had endured so much hardship. But, in some ways, those two objectives were at odds with each other: I could use only cool, neutral colors, which would make the room feel very quiet and peaceful, but if I did that, the masks, all of which are wood, wouldn't have really popped off the walls in the way I wanted them to. So I came up with a compromise. I kept most of the colors in the room neutral, then painted one wall a greenish-turquoise, which contrasted well with the dark wood of the masks but wasn't so brash that it ruined the room's low-key mood. To make the masks on the other wall stand out, I mounted them in shadow boxes, using the same green-tinged turquoise as a background.

Since Veronica's mask collection was fairly exotic, I chose a beautiful teak hardwood to make the bed and other pieces of furniture in the room. It's the combined effect of these exotic wood pieces that gives the room its life and enabled me to keep everything else fairly unembellished. A few dashes of turquoise on the bed and curtains and a couple shapely bedside lamps were all it took to put the final touches on a warm and inviting room.

RIGHT Totem shelves are a great platform for sculptures, vases, and other works of art. And you can make them yourself (see page 218).

OPPOSITE PAGE African masks really pop when perched on a turquoise wall.

FOLLOWING SPREAD It's always safe to stick with a mix of three dominant colors. One of my favorite color combos is turquoise, chocolate brown, and white or cream. Here the threesome provides a warm backdrop for Veronica's African mask collection.

Balancing a Room with Art

When planning your room makeover, you need to take into consideration the room's symmetry: Is it balanced, and what is your wall space like'? Occasionally you'll get rooms with windows that are unevenly spaced or with a single window just sort of hanging there in no man's land. When you do have these imbalances, you can often use art to make up the difference. If you have a long wall that would leave your furniture swimming if you were to center it all in the middle, consider moving the furniture (like a bed and night tables in a bedroom, sofa and side table in a living room) so that it's closer to the end of one wall and balancing it out with something like a big painting; a collection of photos or drawings hung salon style; a sculpture; or even unexpected objects that you treat as art. Maybe it's a vintage bicycle, an old advertising sign, some African drums and shakers that you hang on the wall, a surfboard with a great pattern airbrushed on top. It could be anything that you think is beautiful as long as it provides balance to the furniture on the other side of the wall.

This technique also works when you've got windows that are out of whack. Use art to provide the missing symmetry.

One other thing to keep in mind about art and symmetry: when hanging paintings and photographs, don't go any higher than the top of the room's window frames. In most cases, going higher will disturb the balance of the room and even make the room seem smaller. Usually all the windows will be the same height; if not, use the highest frame as your margin and line up your art either at or below it.

High Contrast

When I was a kid growing up, my family lived in a single-story house that was laid out in a very *Brady Bunch* style. I can picture myself hanging out on the white shag carpet, contemplating the black-and-white Beatles' *Revolver* album cover as I listened along, then looking up at the long black-and-white curtains that hung in our living room. The curtains had a wavy pattern to them and I was amazed when, many years later, I found the exact same curtains in a thrift shop. I immediately purchased two sets, put up one set in my house, then tucked another set away **because, well, you never know.**

ABOVE Keeping everything black and white gives this bedroom a clean, crisp look and makes it a respite from the six toddlers running around on the other side of the door.

OPPOSITE PAGE Contrasting patterns warm up what might otherwise be an austere room. The Gee's Bend quilters used several different black-and-white fabrics to create the Harris's quilt, including a wild, swirly curtain panel exactly like the ones my family owned in the '70s.

As much as I'm crazy about color, I love the stark contrast of black against white, too. And depending on how you put black and white to use, it can look really mod or extremely elegant. A good example of the latter is a room I did for the parents of sextuplets—four of them boys. At the time we arrived to help out the family, the kids were two years old. On the morning we came to the house to kick off the makeover—a hurricane had sent a tree crashing through the living room, one of several reasons the family was in need of help—all six of the kids came flying out the door at the sound of my "Good morning, Harris family!" and just took off. I was yelling at them through the bullhorn and they ignored me! So you can imagine what it was like for their parents day in and day out.

I got the idea to create an all black-and-white room for the Harrises when I discovered that the mom, like me, had a penchant for stark contrasts. I love the intensity of a black-and-white Ansel Adams photograph on a wall, a white flower in a black vase, and a black-ink Japanese dry brush painting. It's all good.

The combination of black and white, it should be mentioned, has the potential to look a little cold, but there are lots of ways to warm it up. In the Harris bedroom I did that by mixing lots of patterns. I covered the chairs in a houndstooth check, covered the walls with paisley wallpaper and scattered pillows in a bold, flowered print around the room. The highlight, though, is the quilt on the bed, which was created especially for the Harrises by renowned quilters from Gee's Bend, Alabama. These African-American women, many of them descendants of slaves, carry on a tradition that's been passed on for generations. Their work is so admired that it's been shown in the Whitney Museum of American Art in New York City and now adorns a stamp. I gave them a panel of the black-and-white curtains I'd found

in the thrift shop and that became the edging of the quilt. And let me tell you, that quilt is absolutely awesome! Perched atop the Harrises' four-poster bed, it's a work of art (and source of warmth).

I also did a similarly graphic, if not entirely black-and-white room, for a great couple in North Carolina. Linda Riggins, despite being told that she wouldn't amount to much, put herself through college and graduated with honors. She started a community center to help keep disadvantaged children in school and offer them activities like music and dance. She and her husband, William devoted over fifteen years to the center. They are beacons of the community and amazing human beings.

Linda has had some medical problems that forced the family to fall on hard times, and William has some problems of his own: He is visually impaired. He can, however, make out shapes. So I decided to create a very graphic room that both Linda and William could enjoy. The black bed, for instance, contrasts with the white bedding and pops off both the yellow headboard wall and gray-and-black paisley wallpaper. The art, too, is meant to stand in high contrast against the walls and it's mostly made up of large botanicals that William can see.

For all their troubles, Linda and William are two joyous people and they certainly brought a lot of joy to the neighborhood. If there was to be a color that represents them it had to be yellow—using it as an accent here was a no-brainer. My favorite part of the room is an ornate bench, now also yellow, that William calls his prayer couch. I think that they had found it in a thrift store and it was pretty beat up before we reupholstered and painted it. The bench has always been a place for William to sit and think late at night; now it's a lot more comfortable spot for contemplation.

I did a third black-and-white room for an *EMHE* family, but before I tell you about it, let me ask you a question: Do you believe in haunted houses?

I didn't think I did until I met the Ray-Smith family. Brittany Ray and Ron Smith, two teachers,

ABOVE Placing art against busy wallpaper can be tricky. These prints work because they're big and bold, which sets them off from their backdrop.

OPPOSITE PAGE Before you toss out an old piece of furniture, consider what a little paint and reupholstering can do. William's rejuvenated prayer bench is set against walls also given a new lease on life with the simple addition of white molding.

FOLLOWING SPREAD With its four-poster bed and paisley bedding, this room has a traditional feel. What makes it modern is its strong graphic quality and the surprising pop of yellow running throughout.

live with their three children in an old house in Maine that was once occupied by Brittany's great-great-grandfather. What we were dealing with first and foremost was the condition of the house. It just wasn't safe for the kids, one of whom is autistic. The repairs were particularly important because the Ray-Smiths were in the process of adopting a daughter from China.

We had been told strange things had happened in the house. It was thought to be haunted and it didn't seem like a good idea to just tear it down without making sure it wouldn't stir up spirits. The Ray-Smiths' safety (and the safety of our crew) was at stake. So we did the logical thing and brought in a medium.

Channeling Brittany's ancestors, the medium told us we had better renovate rather than demolish the house. Then he began to dole out some personal advice to some of us from the "ghosts" in the room. None of my ancestors seemed to be in the room so I asked, "What am I, chopped liver?" in my usual joking way. "Oh, *you've* got some issues," he replied, looking serious.

I would have just laughed it off if he hadn't said that there was someone named George in the room. He could only have been referring to "Big Daddy George," my grandfather. The medium went on to tell me things about my family history that there was no way he could have known. Let me tell you, it was eerie. And that was only a tidbit of the bizarre stuff that started happening on that project.

I worked on Brittany and Ron's room, taking my cue from something Brittany had told me. She said that she had always seen the world in black and white, very clean and simple, until she had a child with autism. Then things got muted and gray. To give her back some of that simplicity, I stuck to a largely black-and-white palette anchored by graphic wallpaper adorned with bare trees. To give the trees some life, I added some cutouts of ravens, birds I'd seen lining up on the side of the road on the way to the house. Now here's the other twisted thing. When

Brittany saw the room and the wallpaper in particular she asked me, "How did you know?" Turns out, her grandfather used to tell her that her ancestors would come back to watch over her in the form of ravens. Spooky!

Black-and-white bedrooms are not for the meek—they make a pretty strong design statement. But there are other, subtler ways to use a graphic look to good effect. Usually pop comes from a bolt of color set against a mostly neutral background; but the reverse works, too: a bolt of black and white set against a more colorful background. A good example of this is a bedroom I designed for a New York policeman named John Vitale. John's wife died tragically of leukemia at the age of twenty-eight, leaving him alone with three boys under the age of five. The family had been in the process of renovating their home when John's wife got sick and hospital and burial costs ate up all their renovation funds. *EMHE* decided to finish the job for them, and I had the good fortune to create a new bedroom for John.

Because I wanted the room to have a masculine vibe, I kept the colors fairly low key—the bedding and side chairs are mostly in autumny red and orange hues—and used wood to add rich tones to the mix. The floor is natural maple, the bed and two bedside tables I custom designed are made from a dark walnut and the tongue-and-groove flooring on the back wall is walnut, too, stained an even darker, espresso brown. To get a better sense of John, I had asked him, "What do you love in life?" and his answer was this: "I love waking up every day to my kids and seeing their faces." I took what he said to heart. I photographed the boys and blew up the pictures, mounted them, and created a montage of six black-and-white photos that now hang above John's dresser. The photos are really striking, not only because they contrast with the colors in the room, but because they're hung a few inches away from the wall (I used a French cleat, which causes them to jut out slightly). The kids literally leap out at John when he opens up his eyes in the morning.

ABOVE It's always nice to have a "clothes" chair in a bedroom, a place to dump your clothes when you're so tired all you want to do is climb into bed. But even if you're going to cover it up half the time, choose a good-looking chair. This red one might be tucked in the corner, but it's no wallflower.

OPPOSITE PAGE Set against a colorful backdrop, the black-and-white faces of the Vitale children are striking and add great feeling to their father's bedroom. The bedding is understated enough to be masculine but still colorful enough to add energy.

Lighting
the Way

Lighting is everything. Trust me, I have to see myself on television every day so I'm all too familiar with the good, the bad, and the ugly effects of lighting. You could be a Brazilian swimsuit model but, in the wrong light, look like a Halloween nightmare. The lighting you choose for your bedroom is going to affect the way *everything* in it looks, from the art to the color of the walls to your own smiling face. So don't give it short shrift. Lighting deserves your attention not as an afterthought, but as a prime component of your design.

Lighting played an important role in a bedroom I designed for two police officers in Southern California, Kristina Rapatti and Tim Pearce.

The backstory: Tim and Kristina met while in police training, were partners for a while, fell in love, got married, and had a baby daughter. One morning Kristina got up, ran a relay race to raise money to support the families of deceased police officers, then went to work (she patrolled one of the most gang-ridden and dangerous areas of L.A.). While cruising the neighborhood, she and her partner saw a suspicious-looking character, who turned out to have just robbed a store. As Kristina chased him down, the man spun around and shot her, severing her spine. As she waited for help, Tim heard the call on his radio and rushed over to find his wife on the ground, her life hanging by a thread.

If Kristina had not been so athletic—besides surfing every other day, she used to run seven miles to the gym, work out, then run home again—she might not have made it. As it is, she is now confined to a wheelchair and paralyzed from the chest down. Kristina, who would fearlessly go out there among murderers to protect us citizens, now fears that she can't protect her own toddler-age daughter or be the mom she has always wanted to be.

The greatest thing about building a new house for this family was knowing that, by outfitting it with all the latest designs for people with disabilities, we were going to give Kristina back some of her autonomy (she'd been sleeping in a hospital bed in the living room). Although it looks pretty much like a regular bedroom, Kristina and Tim's room actually has lots of helpful gadgetry so that Kristina doesn't have to constantly be dependent on others. Just as important, the room is *expansive*. By that I mean, not that the room is especially roomy (although it is very uncluttered), but that it references the world outside and, more specifically, the ocean, which is Kristina's great love. While she may not be able to go to the beach as much as she used to, at least she

ABOVE A strip of halogen bulbs is recessed behind a panel at the top of the wall.

OPPOSITE PAGE While you wouldn't know it to look at it, the bed in this room is adjusts like a hospital bed to make it easier for Kristina to get in and out.

INSET Clockwise from left: Police officer Tim Pearce, me, his mother Jean Pearce, Kristina Rapatti, and Jordan Pearce.

doesn't have to feel stuck at home looking at four dreary walls.

All the walls of Tim's and her room reference the ocean in some way. Two were painted sea blue, one was covered in sea grass wallpaper and accented with a driftwood mantle, and all three walls were hung with photographs of children playing in the surf. Then there's the one I like to call the "wave wall." It's a sculptural wall inspired by the ripples of sand that form on the ocean floor. After designing the wall, I called in a crew of friends who helped me shape the waves using wire mesh and a substance called vermiculite, which we smoothed over with plaster. (Vermiculite is a naturally occurring mineral that kind of acts like a cross between plaster and Styrofoam. It's often used for insulation. If you're interested in trying something like this, I recommend getting an expert wall plasterer to help you.)

The lighting of the wave wall was key to getting the whole effect. I installed a strip of halogen bulbs at the top and hid them behind a panel painted white to match the wall. The lights really accentuate the wall's depth and texture. Because the bulbs are on a dimmer, the couple can raise and lower the brightness.

Being able to adjust the mood of the room was something that seemed like it might be important to Kristina, who told me that she wanted a room to be a retreat when she was having a bad day. That was understandable, but what I really wanted to do was give her a room where she could have a good day. And that meant giving her a room that would enable her to be independent and lift her mood when she was feeling low.

Oddly enough, while we were working away on the wall, Kristina, Tim, and their daughter were on vacation in Baja California, where they took a ride in a glass-bottom boat and spent some time admiring the natural ridges the water created in the sand. When they came home and saw the wave wall, Kristina knew exactly what it represented and she loved it. And I loved that she loved it. What could be better than making someone who is truly a hero happy?

OPPOSITE PAGE The wave wall not only brings in the feel of the ocean but also gives the room light and depth.

The Bedroom Accent Wall

In just about every room, there's one wall that immediately draws the eye. That's the accent wall, which, in most of the bedrooms I design is a term that's interchangeable with "the wall the bed is on." (But "accent wall" sounds a lot more interior design-y, don't you think?) In any case, creating some drama on one wall in particular is a sure way to give a bedroom some personality. And there are several different ways to do it.

The first step, of course, is to choose which wall you're going to highlight. Often that choice is dictated by the architectural layout of the room. When there are two windows on a wall with generous space between them, I generally like to place the bed right in the middle, which creates automatic symmetry and balance (see Veronica Ginyard's room on pages 62–63). Often, though, a room's layout isn't so obviously balanced, so you have to get creative. The way I approached the problem in Sadie Holmes's room (opposite and page 96) was by creating wall art in place of a headboard. In this room, the obvious place to put the bed was on a very long, windowless wall, however, I didn't want to let the bed just float in empty space. Placing the paper "waterfall" behind it, defines the space and adds drama.

There are tons of ways to define the accent bedroom wall. Installing a bed with a great-looking headboard is probably the simplest, but you'll still need to add something to make it pop, whether it's painting the wall a different color than the rest of the room or covering the wall with wallpaper. Another great way to define a wall is to cover it with tongue-and-groove flooring. This works particularly well for a masculine room, like the one I did for John Vitale (page 79). Also don't underestimate the impact of an excellent piece of art hanging above the bed. And a four-poster bed creates its own sort of drama; you don't have to worry

about the wall if you've got a stunning bed set against it.

If you don't have a bed with an interesting headboard and aren't inclined to invest in one, you can always create a detached headboard and attach it to the wall with a French cleat (two interlocking pieces of wood, one attached to the wall, the other to the object you're hanging). For instance, in a bedroom I designed for a Marine, I used a router to cut out stars in a 7' x 8' wood headboard (it fell behind both the bed and the bedside tables). But it doesn't have to be that elaborate. Using a staple gun, you can also cover a board with foam and fabric to make a plush and elegant headboard. There is no end to the possibilities. Just make sure you use that French cleat or some other means of attaching the headboard to the wall (especially if you live in earthquake country). You don't want it falling on you in the middle of the night.

Another place where I was able to use lighting to good effect was in a bedroom I did for Patricia Broadbent, an AIDS activist and adoptive mother of six children, some of whom are HIV-positive. Patricia is an incredible optimist, who has taught her children to go out and have a full life despite their health status. A former social worker, she has also helped raise awareness about the AIDS crisis and its effect on children. In the midst of all these selfless efforts, Patricia was diagnosed with lung cancer and, when the *EMHE* team met her, she was undergoing chemotherapy. It was clear, then, that she needed a bedroom where she could not only decompress from the work she was doing in the community, but where she could rest and recover. To that end, I thought her room should have the same qualities as a spa: Zenlike calm and a simple, clean-lined design that, while spare, is not austere. The best spas are warm and nurturing, which is exactly how I wanted Patricia's room to feel.

We made it happen by using strategic lighting to set off the earthy colors and textiles and highlight the room's natural beauty. Behind Patricia's bed, for instance, are two floor-to-ceiling panels made of eco-resin, a non-toxic, translucent substance made largely of recycled materials. (You can find it through the Web site www.3-form.com/index.php.) The panels have fibers running through them that give the *illusion* of texture, but because they're "swimming" in a polymer, the fibers don't collect dust the way something with real texture, like a tapestry, does. To give the resin a glow and cause the fibers to pop, I placed small directional lights above the panels, just as if I was showing off a painting.

Certain types of lamps can also add warm radiance to a room and, if you have any interest in do-it-yourself projects, lamps are especially easy to make. Plus, you can turn all kinds of unconventional objects into lampshades: the lights flanking Patricia's bed were created out of Chinese neck pillows, which look like curved wicker baskets. Because they're flammable, I had to use low-wattage bulbs (don't try this at home with halogen bulbs—the lamps will catch fire, and that's not good!), but that wasn't a problem: The low lights enhanced the peaceful atmosphere of the room. It's also easy to make a lamp with wood veneer as a shade. It's simply a matter of constructing a base out of a couple sticks of wood, then shaping a strip of veneer into a circle, and glueing it together. (See page 214 for the how-to.) The lightbulb illuminates the grain of the veneer, and your simple lamp becomes a thing of beauty.

OPPOSITE PAGE Frankly, I don't think this Chinese neck pillow looks too comfortable, but it makes a great-looking table lamp. When it comes to lighting, use your imagination—almost anything, from colanders to funnels, can be turned into a lamp.

PRECEDING SPREAD To get a look reminiscent of a spa, opt for natural tones and soft lighting. The lights above the bed are on a dimmer, an inexpensive device that lets you control the mood of a room. I recommend putting dimmer switches on almost every lamp and overhead light so you always have control over a room's brightness.

Luxury and Elegance

Luxury and **elegance** are not two words you'd usually associate with me (it's okay; I know I'm a down-home kind of guy), but I can rise to the occasion. In fact, because I've traveled so much and spent many nights in hotel rooms, I've gotten to know more about luxury and elegance than I ever dreamed possible. (I've also gotten to know more about crummy motel rooms than I've ever dreamed possible, but that's another story.)

TOP The headboard was designed to echo the pattern on the bedding, a beaded design in my line for Sears called "Origami." Next to the bed, cylindrical hanging lights take the place of traditional table lamps, freeing up the bedside tables for books (and all the other stuff that inevitably creeps onto them). The crunchy sisal rug under the bed provides a nice contrast to the bed's glossy finish. The wallpaper chosen for this room reminded me of the gardenias in the yard.

BOTTOM If you're going to make a bed yourself, choose wood with a beautiful grain. This headboard is made from teak carved using a routing machine.

OPPOSITE PAGE I'm partial to adding strips of color to beds. Here it's beaded bands of dusty green at the foot and on the pillows.

W hen I was presented with the task of designing a room for Bruce and Paulita Lewis, a California couple dealing with a tremendous amount of hardship, I wanted to capture the feel of a chic hotel room. Paulita was battling stage IV cancer and she really needed a clean, serene, and beautiful place to recover from her grueling treatments. Ultimately, Paulita passed away but I hope that by creating a beautiful room with an air-cleansing HEPA filter, we helped extend her life a little bit.

Paulita definitely deserved some indulgences. After a remodel of their home went sour, Bruce and Paulita along with their two children (and the most massive cat I have ever seen—that thing was the size of a toddler) were all living in a small room in Bruce's mother's apartment. Not only was the work on their house shoddy—rain eventually caved in the roof—but also the contractor left town with $40,000 of the family's money.

One of the first things that came to mind when I was contemplating my design for Bruce and Paulita's bedroom was wallpaper. Wallpaper gives a room a very "finished" look and, depending on the pattern you choose, can add instant elegance. Sure, there are some scary wallpapers out there (I have had nightmares about being trapped between four walls of cloying cabbage roses), but there are also some great, very modern patterns available. The wallpaper I ended up using in the Lewises' room is floral, but not overly sweet, and its light metallic sheen makes it look modern and, not incidentally, gives the room an incandescent glow.

In some ways, wallpaper can limit your options when it comes to furnishings and bedding—you don't want to bring too many other patterns into the mix or you'll wind up with sensory overload. But that doesn't mean you can't bring in any other patterns at all. In the Lewises' room, a headboard with an interlocking cutout design abuts the wallpaper, but the combination works because the wood is neutral

and the pattern isn't too ornate. I also brought in one more pattern—the beaded embroidery on the bedding—though only as an accent. Had the whole bed been covered in the pattern, it would have been a little too much.

Another thing to keep in mind about wallpaper is that there's no rule that says you have to cover an entire wall. In a room I created for a woman named Sadie Holmes, I applied it in swaths interspersed with chocolate brown paint. Like a lot of wallpapers, this one—a bonsai tree pattern in white and mint green—even though it's extremely elegant, had the potential to be overbearing. Breaking it up into sections ensured that it wouldn't overwhelm everything else in the room.

Sadie is another one of the many women for whom I've had the pleasure of designing that really deserved some luxury in her life. A former drug addict, she turned her life around when she found that she was in danger of losing her children. The people in her community were so proud of Sadie that they donated all kinds of food, clothing, and furniture to help her. Soon she had so much that she decided to give it out to other people in need, and the next thing you know, she'd found her calling: running a distribution center for homeless people who needed a new start. When a hurricane hit their Florida town, the home where Sadie and her family lived was badly damaged. Then a fire damaged it even further. By the time we came along, the family was in dire straits.

So it was a great feeling to give Sadie an extravagant, lush, and comfortable room. I used the wallpaper as a jumping-off point so the room is somewhat Asian in flavor. But I also wanted to give it a bit of a twist, and that's where the "waterfall" came in: What looks like a textured wall is really just pieces of paper folded on top of each other and glued on to pieces of mounted plywood. Lightly written on each piece of paper are the names of the people who pitched in to build the Holmeses' new house.

I'm all for adding something unexpected to make a room distinctive. In Sadie's room it was the paper

TOP Sadie turned over a new leaf. Here, I hand-painted a literal interpretation of her transformation.

BOTTOM I found this bonsai tree wallpaper for Sadie's room, then serendipitously found fabric in a very similar pattern. Extra wallpaper was used to cover books.

OPPOSITE PAGE With the paper waterfall on the headboard wall, there was a lot going on in this room so the trick was to keep the cumulative effect from becoming overwhelming. The solution was to confine the patterns I added to the room to strips. For instance, instead of blanketing the wall with wallpaper, I hung it in wide panels. Likewise, the patterned fabric on the bedding is confined to a horizontal strip with a few smaller strips on the throw pillows.

waterfall. In a bedroom I did for a teenager named Gina, it was intentionally going over the top with the use of molding.

Gina is the daughter of a firefighter and local hero who adopted two neighborhood children when they were facing the possibility of being sent to foster homes. This raised the total number of males in Gina's family to five and left her as the only girl in the household. So I wanted to make her bedroom not just luxurious and feminine, but also reminiscent of something that every woman I know loves: a posh hotel room, and in this case, one with some European charm.

Whether you're going for the hotel room look or not, molding is a great way to give an ordinary space architectural detail and a little French flair. But because Gina was only thirteen, I didn't want the room to be too serious. So instead of the traditional approach of placing a few molding "boxes" on the walls, I went a little wild and put them pretty much everywhere, including the headboard of the cherry bed I built for her. I have to admit, it was a labor-intensive endeavor—creating those boxes entailed carefully cutting tons of molding (which you can purchase at home improvement stores) and measuring and leveling like mad to make sure that everything lined up perfectly on the wall—but the outcome made it worthwhile.

While the molding gives Gina's room both wit and sophistication, the details are just plain sophisticated. I painted a big elegant *G* on the ceiling to bring attention to its height, then had the same design embroidered on two throw pillows. Instead of table lamps, Gina now has charming sconces to read by and a sunburst mirror where there might have otherwise been a poster. The room, though, still has certain elements of simplicity. There are really only three colors—green, pink, and white—and the furnishings are clean-lined and outfitted with plain hardware. Luxury, after all, isn't about how elaborate you can make a room, but rather about the quality of the things you place there. Even when you're doing a room that's far from minimalist, less is generally more.

ABOVE Who said shelves must have parallel lines? Angled sides add humor to the room and help remind all who enter that a budding teenager lives here.

OPPOSITE PAGE Since the giant letter *G* was painted where a light fixture would typically reside, recessed can lights were installed around the perimeter of the ceiling and sconces placed on either side of the bed. To create the *G*, I worked out the font on my computer, then printed it out on thin paper. Next, I traced the letter on the back of the paper with a carpenter's pencil, then to apply it, I flipped it over and rubbed it on the ceiling. That gave me the lines to follow, which I just painted over in red. Putting molding on the wall isn't the easiest do-it-yourself job—it involves lots of measuring and cutting—but the end result makes it well worth it (then again, so is hiring a pro to do it).

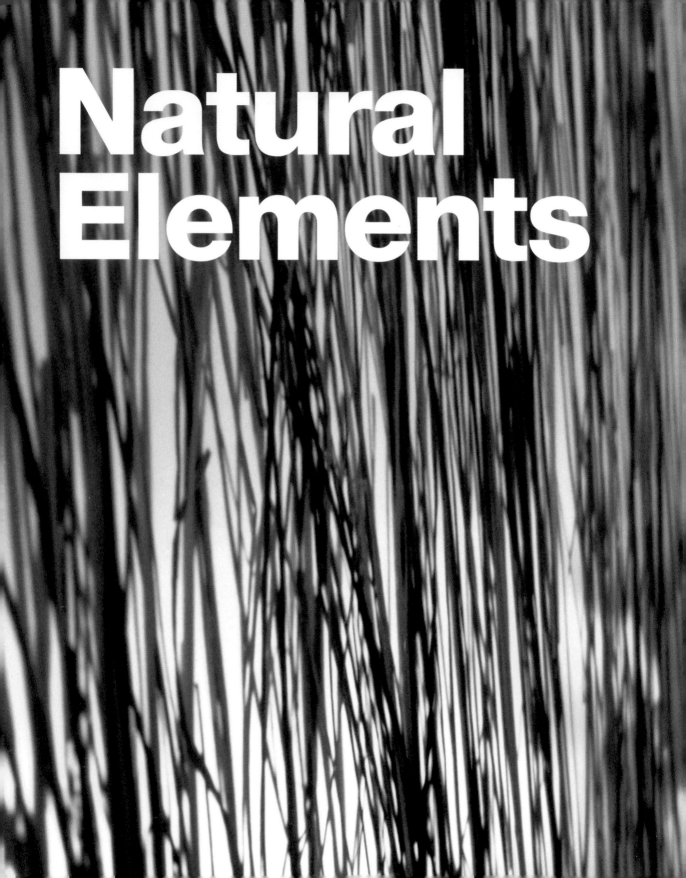

Natural
Elements

Just about every room benefits from a touch of nature, whether it's a living, breathing house-plant, a landscape painting, or just a collection of interesting rocks arranged on a shelf. Natural elements symbolize growth and renewal and are great reminders that life is cyclical: Just as the seasons go from dreary to light, lives marked by misfortune also inevitably brighten. But enough with the metaphors. **Nature is a treasure trove of beautiful things!** Why not borrow some of them to give a room style?

There are a couple of ways to go about bringing the outdoors in. One is to borrow from the environment that surrounds your home. That's pretty much what I did when I created a bedroom for a Native American couple in Flagstaff, Arizona. I basically went "shopping" right outside the family's door in order to build some of the furnishings in the room. I let the gorgeous landscape serve as my inspiration. Flying into Arizona, I was taken by dramatic shifts in landscape, from the flat red earth to the dusty brown canyons to the snow-capped peaks, and knew that I wanted to somehow capture that same feeling in this wonderful couple's room. I also wanted to draw on the family's Native American heritage, which I knew was an important part of its identity. Luckily, of course, my two sources of inspiration were not incompatible because so much of Native American symbolism is grounded in an appreciation for the earth.

ABOVE Native Americans perform a traditional Hopi dance with the Arizona mountains as a backdrop.

OPPOSITE PAGE The colors used in this room—sand tones, deep reds, and oranges—reflect the local terrain. With all the Navajo blankets and Native American crafts in the room, I didn't bother hanging any artwork on the wall. That would have been overkill.

EMHE had learned about the couple, Percy and Terry Piestewa, from former POW Jessica Lynch. Lynch's roommate and best friend was the Piestewases' daughter, PFC Lori Piestewa, who was the first American woman killed in Iraq. Jessica and Lori had a pact that each would take care of the other's family if something happened to them. Lori was only twenty-three when she died, and she left behind a young son and daughter, now being raised by Percy and Terry. When we first met the family, they were living in a mobile home (that, frankly, had seen better days) in Tuba City, hoping to move to Flagstaff so they could be closer to relatives.

I almost always start any design with whatever's going to be the impact piece, and in a bedroom that's usually the bed. For the Piestewas, I built a detached headboard for the simple platform bed from indigenous trees. The headboard, with its rough-hewn, unfinished timber is meant to recapture the connection between the wood in our homes and the trees it comes from—and not, if you'll forgive the pun, fade into the woodwork. I also used local wood to create two "teepee" lamps, a mantle over the fireplace, and the rungs of which are a ladder for hanging handcrafted Native American blankets. The room didn't really need any wall art, because it had so much in the way of artful crafts, including a rustic twig basket filled with red, black, yellow, and white corn (symbolizing human beings of different colors living together) made by a Hopi woman who's a friend of the Piestewas.

While the Piestewa room echoed the world outside their doors, a bedroom I did for Beverly Turner echoed a place she couldn't get to so easily— the beach. Beverly has been the adoptive mother to eighteen kids with special needs. Despite suffering from a neuromuscular disease, she is raising kids with many different disabilities, including autism, bipolar disorder, and blindness by herself. Many of her kids were also abused or neglected at one time in their early lives.

ABOVE Starfish and sand dollars serve as objets d'art.

OPPOSITE PAGE The inspiration for this bedding was a tile floor I saw in a Cuban restaurant in New York City. To create the mural, we sketched organic shapes on the wall, then came back and filled in color with a paintbrush.

In 2005, Beverly's New Jersey home burned down in a fire caused by faulty wiring, and she and the nine children living with her then were left to the mercy of friends and family. The community was so moved by her plight that one hundred people (including the mayor) clipped an article in the paper about the fire and sent it to us. Creating a little sanctuary for Beverly was my job.

Not surprisingly, this is a woman who rarely gets any down time. "Sometimes I sit on my bed and read two pages of a book, then I'm good to go again," she told me. Wow, I thought, she has an amazing amount of energy. Yet operating on the premise that if she had a nicer place to have a time out, she might be inspired to give herself more of a break, I set out to create a tranquil space for Beverly. And since she'd told me that she loves the beach but didn't get there very often, I decided to bring the beach—or at least a beachy feeling—to her.

If you want to use nature as your inspiration, you don't necessarily have to be literal. While I did scatter some bleached starfish, shells, and sand dollars around, everything else in the room is meant to evoke water and sand. For instance, I painted the walls a cool, cool turquoise reminiscent of the Caribbean sea, and hand painted organic forms that resembled seaweed or coral. The rest of the room is done in varying sand tones with some deeper browns and blues for accents. There's enough color in the room to keep it from looking washed out, but because the colors largely fall within just two families, blue and brown, it still has a relaxing quality—just like the sand and the sea.

As you can tell from much of the furniture I design and build, I have a thing for beautiful wood. Jeff Novak has a thing for trees, or more specifically, the Celtic tree of life, a symbol that he had tattooed on his arm after the death of his wife, Jackie. Jackie, just twenty-eight, died in her sleep of a pulmonary embolism, strangely enough, the same night that they had watched our show and she had told Jeff she was going to figure out a way to get us to come

OPPOSITE PAGE When I asked Jeff's daughter Zoe what she wanted us to do to her home, she said, "Make my dad happy" and started crying. That tore my heart out. The greatest art of all—Jeff's three beautiful daughters, larger than life.

ABOVE A ring that Jeff gave Jackie encased in an illuminated niche cut into the wall.

OPPOSITE PAGE Furnishings and a floor made from deep, rich walnut give the room an earthy and masculine feel. Ecoresin fibers running through the headboard look like tall grass.

over and make over their house (it was in pretty bad shape). The couple had three daughters, the youngest of whom was just a few months old when Jackie passed away.

I took on the task of giving Jeff, a special education teacher, a new bedroom that would honor Jackie but also give him a chance to move on with his life. The tree, I thought, was the perfect jumping-off point since it was emblematic of both growth and strength, two things he was going to need in the coming months. So not only did I put a silk screen of the Celtic tree of life over Jeff's bed, I outfitted the room in deep rich walnut. I chose wood where the grain was readily apparent so that the bed, the dresser, and the floor had a very organic look. On one side of the room, I cut a rectangular recess into the wall and illuminated it—a great thing to do when you want to display something special but don't have a mantle. (Another alternative is to buy a floating wall shelf, which you screw into the wall.) Inside the niche is a tree branch with changing leaves, a picture of Jackie, and a ring that Jeff had given her.

In keeping with the organic look of the room, all the colors, mostly oranges, yellows, and browns, are also very natural. And while the tie-dyed bedding isn't something you actually see in nature, it does have a whole-earth quality to it. There's a story behind it, too. One of the things that Jeff and Jackie shared was a love of both the Grateful Dead and reggae music. And like all good Deadheads, they loved tie-dye— Jackie was planning to teach the technique to kids at her school (she, too, was a teacher). When she died she was wearing a tie-dyed Bob Marley T-shirt, which had to be cut off by the EMS technicians as they tried to save her. Jeff had Jackie's mom make the T-shirt into a pillow and I took it a step further, letting it inspire the bedding for his room. Finally, I took some pictures of Jeff's kids and produced them in a sepia tone. My favorite one is of little Presley sticking out her tongue. It's almost as if it's Jackie herself saying, it's okay, life is funny, you never know what it's going to throw at you.

Recycling

Recycling is on just about everyone's radar now, and that's a great thing. I'm a big fan of recycling. In fact, I not only believe in recycling, I believe in reincarnation. Now, by "reincarnation," I mean giving something that you might otherwise throw out or give away a completely new life.

We often get rid of objects and furnishings that have outlived their original purpose, and sometimes that's the right thing to do. They need to go. But some things—in fact, many things—can be turned into something else. I've even made lamps out of plungers. Of course, I'm not the only one rethinking old junk. In Africa, they make baskets out of old telephone wire and other garbage to sell to tourists. I've seen beautiful placemats made from old garbage bags and awesome rugs made out of old T-shirts. So before you throw away anything, try to rethink it; you never know what you might come up with.

Maybe you've got an old bedspread that can be made into pillows or used as a border to offset photographs in a frame. Maybe you can take the decorative top off an old bookshelf, and paint it a shade that jibes with the new colors you want to put into the room. Maybe you can remove the doors from an armoire and put shelves inside to create a bookcase.

BELOW Posts from the front porch were cut down and paired with new plywood to make matching twin beds. To create the room's mural, the pattern was projected on the wall, the outlines traced, and the colors filled in.

OPPOSITE PAGE Recycled and whitewashed pine planks were used to make this bedroom feel like a cottage.

If there's nothing in the room you can salvage, take a tour through your garage to see if there's anything you shoved in there a while back that can be fixed up and repurposed. Check garage sales and flea markets for old items you might be able to make work in unexpected ways. Hell, I'm not above hauling something I see on garbage day off the street if I think I can turn it into something great. One man's trash is another man's treasure, after all.

One of my best flea market finds was a set of antique riddling racks. These beautiful oak racks, which have circular cutouts covering their surfaces, were once used in the making of champagne. The bottles were angled into the holes to keep the corks wet and on tight and to allow the wine makers to routinely turn the bottles, keeping sediment from settling. The racks generally sit on the floor, angled against each other like a sandwich board, but I've separated them to create headboards and used them as wall hangings, like pieces of art.

TOP The more mural painters you've got, the merrier.

BOTTOM These rustic, Japanese-style lamps are made from recycled lathe. See page 214 to learn how to make them.

OPPOSITE PAGE My producers worried that the mural pattern my team and I painted on the wall would be too wild for the family. Turns out the pattern, inspired by bandanas, so ubiquitous in this part of the country, made them feel right at home.

With a little imagination, there is no end to the ways you can recycle. Here's another example. When we built a new home for a family in Colorado, I took posts from the porch of the old house and reused them as bedposts (peeling paint and all). I also cut up some of the scraps and used them as candleholders. Some of the lathe—small pieces of wood used in the interior of the old walls—were reassembled to create small table lamps.

In this case, giving something that seemed unusable a new lease on life had particular meaning since it was created for a husband and wife who've dedicated their lives to doing the same thing with animals and children. Billy Jack and Anne Barrett are horse whisperers, known for their gentle approach to training mistrustful horses and, now, for success in helping mistrustful children feel confident and loved. Their work with children started when a friend brought a child who was living in a foster home and having a hard time to see the horses trained by Billy Jack and Anne. The Barretts ended up adopting not only that boy, but three other kids who'd been in and out of foster homes and were considered "unmanageable."

Our quest was to give the Barrett family (the couple also has two biological children) a larger house so that they'd have room to adopt even more kids—in fact, I dubbed the bedroom I designed "a little more room." When Billy Jack saw the room, he recognized the posts from the old house immediately. "The people who'd built the original house were friends of ours. They're so happy that you used some of the original pieces because they put their heart and soul into building the house," he said. "You have no idea how much it means to me."

Wood is one of the best materials of all to recycle. Even old planks can get a second life. For one project, I used them as paneling, whitewashing them to give the room a vintage-y, cottage-y feel. It's an easy process: First, you rub the planks with steel wool, going with the grain, to create little grooves in the wood that will expose the lightest color of the wood. Then, after lightly sanding the planks, whitewash them. The resulting paneling will be very pale, and that will make everything you put in front of it—other, deeper-toned woods, pottery, upholstered furniture—pop.

When I said earlier that there is no end to the ways you can recycle, I meant it. Once I even recycled lasts, the wooden molds that cobblers use to make and repair shoes. I got the idea when *EMHE* was building a new home for the family of Dunstin Rainford, a Jamaican-born man who had just received U.S. citizenship when he was diagnosed with non-Hodgkin's lymphoma. In the midst of his treatment, a hurricane blew the roof off the Florida home Dunstin shared with his kids.

Dunstin had a cobbler's shop in his house where he made shoes as a hobby. He showed me around, and I could tell he was absolutely passionate about his shoes. The only thing more important to him was his kids. Taking that as my cue I did what you might call a little fancy footwork: I took black-and-white photos of his six kids, mounted them on foam core, then placed them in slots I carved into shoe lasts. He was facing a long and uncertain recovery, and I hoped that gazing at the faces he loved might give him strength.

OPPOSITE PAGE TOP Dunstin's walls are hung with ceramic casts of his children's feet.

OPPOSITE PAGE BOTTOM Cleverly reused, both everyday and industrial objects can become things of beauty. Here, shoe lasts sub for picture frames. A shoe last can also be made into a lamp base.

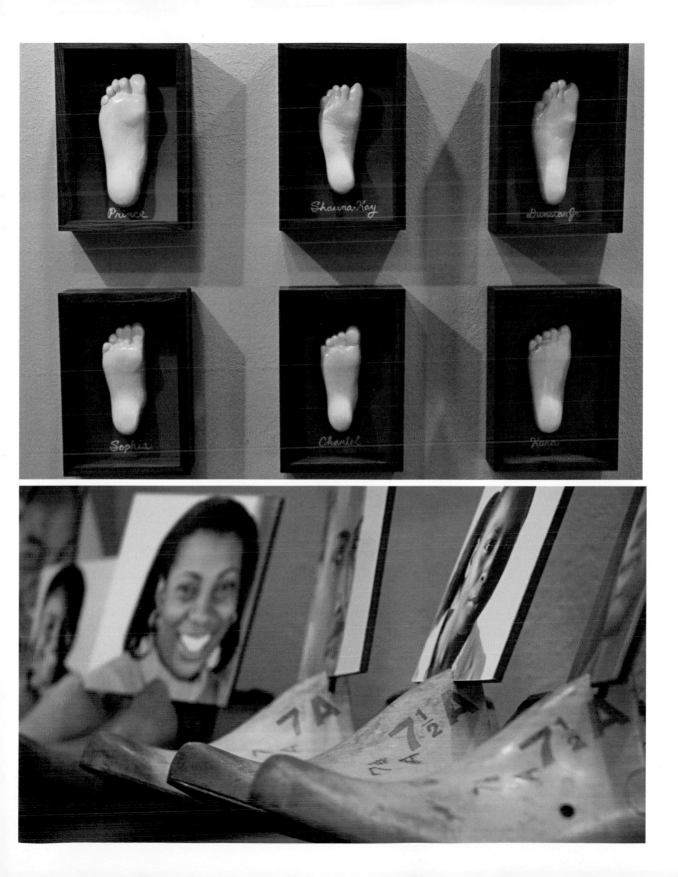

Rooms to Grow in

As a kid I asked a lot of questions, the main one being "Why?" Ty, it's time for bed. "Why?" Time for dinner. "Why?" Usually I'd be told, You'll understand when you get older, which is sort of code for, You should understand right now that it's because I said so. But the beauty of being a kid is that you don't have to understand or worry about anything. You don't have to worry about bills, work, the world's problems, or even your own family's problems. Or at least you shouldn't. The sad truth of it is, though, that for many of the kids for whom I've designed rooms, life is full of worry. Still, **when you're a kid, it's easy to get lost in another, better world if you're given the opportunity.**

ABOVE I used plywood cutouts to trace ovals of varying sizes on the wall, which I then painted in on top of a lime green background. It's one of the easiest ways to craft a mural, and when you use bold colors to fill in the lines, it adds a lot of fresh energy to the room.

I guess that's why I've never wanted to grow up, and it's certainly why I love designing kids' rooms. Kids' rooms are all about fostering a child's fantasies and making a kid's dream of having fun every day come true. And that means that you can pretty much let your imagination run wild. The sky's the limit. Exaggerated colors and motifs? No problem. No need to be subtle. Get a theme and go for it in a big way.

Two of my favorite thematic bedrooms were for young girls battling cancer. These kids were amazing—real fighters—who had the strength that most adults could only hope for. It was a great privilege to design their rooms. Each space was designed not only to be healthy—we used all nontoxic materials—but to lift their spirits in the hopes that it would aid in their recovery. For Tara, that meant a room that was all about butterflies. For Kassandra, it was an indoor garden, complete with (faux) grass and a giant bug.

Tara, who was seven when we met her, had leukemia. Both she and her identical twin sister Sara were first diagnosed with the disease when they were two. Both girls went into remission, but Tara got sick again and had to undergo a bone marrow transplant. While she was recovering, we came in and demolished her family's single-wide trailer and built a new, spacious home where Tara could have her own room (to stay well, she needed to be separated from her three other siblings to reduce the risk of infection).

I went to visit Tara in the hospital and noticed that there was a butterfly printed on her pillow. She seemed to like butterflies and it struck me as appropriate that this little girl was drawn to such a potent symbol of change. We talked about what it was like having to go through treatment, and she told me that she was scared she would have to go to heaven before her time. It just wrecked me to think that this young girl had to go to sleep each night wondering if she was going to be alive in a week or a month or a year. I wanted to create a room that would let her know how special she was and where she could be her best seven-year-old self.

All the furniture I designed for Tara's room had butterfly cutouts. But I didn't stop there (as I said, when it comes to children's rooms, more is more). To create the butterfly mural on the wall, I used a very simple technique. I cut out three sets of plywood ovals to use as stencils for butterfly abstractions on the walls. I had the vibrant mural motif transferred onto the bedding (a seamstress used the same stencils I used on the walls to create a butterfly appliqué) and, for good measure, put a butterfly rug on the floor. I also bought a bunch of itty bitty fake but convincing butterflies and sewed them onto sheer curtain panels so it looked like butterflies were flying all around the room.

I knew that Tara loved having tea parties, so I included a small table and chairs in the room. I glued some of the tiny butterflies on her teacups and teapot, and when she came home from the hospital the two of us had tea. When I asked her what she hoped for the future, she said that she hoped she would stay well. Me, too. I hope Tara spreads her wings and grows up to be a beautiful, healthy adult.

Kassandra was the other little girl fighting for her life. After she was diagnosed with a tumor on her kidney, Kassandra wrote to the show asking us to paint the walls of the hospital where she was being treated. The walls, she noted, were sometimes the last sight some of the kids at the hospital would see. We did paint the hospital walls, but we also wanted to help out Kassandra's family. Her father had lost his truck-driving job for missing work while he visited Kassandra in the hospital. Imagine: You've got six children to support, one of whom is very ill, and you're out of work.

Because of her illness, Kassandra had spent many months indoors, so my mission was to give her a bedroom that would let her experience some aspect of the outdoors. The room I ultimately designed was made to look like a lush garden full of flowers. I also created a mural for Kassandra's room. First, I used a sprayer to paint the wall in graduated shades of green, going from dark at the bottom to light at the top. Then I

ABOVE Plywood works well as a stencil because it stays in place while you trace.

OPPOSITE PAGE I picked up the butterfly theme when building a tea table and chairs.

painted on stems of varying heights, topping some of them with adhesive-backed flowers that I designed on my computer and had printed. (I used the same giant "stickers" on the nightstands I built.)

Doing something interesting and out of the ordinary on the walls of a kid's room transforms it immediately. To take it a step further, you can make the furniture just as fanciful. In Kassandra's room, for instance, her bed is a giant bug. It has big eyes that swivel to create a little shelf for books and antennae that double as reading lights. Not surprisingly, I call it the "bed bug." The room also has a little gazebo that Kassandra can sit in, just as if she were out in the backyard, and a chest for storing her clothes covered

ABOVE I used a paint gun to draw flower stems on the wall; the flower themselves are adhesive-backed.

OPPOSITE PAGE If you're short on space, you might consider buying a bed that has built-in night tables. The bed bug I built for this room has both built-in night tables and gooseneck lamps. Since the room was large enough to accommodate more furniture, I added some small side tables to add space for books and other bedroom paraphernalia.

with "grass" (actually broom bristles painted green) and some enormous paper flowers I found at an art store. Even the hanging lights are made to look like oversized sunflowers.

When Kassandra came into the room for the first time, her eyes lit up. Here was a room that would help her heal while allowing her to feel as though she was outdoors at the same time.

Girls Just Wanna Have Fun

For some reason, my special project often ends up being a little girl's room. I don't know—maybe someone wants me to get in touch with my feminine side. Or maybe I was a girl in another life, Tyra, instead of Ty. Whatever the reason, I see it as a blessing because **nothing is more fun than creating a little world separate from the rest of the house.** Girls tend to like rooms that are rich in fantasy, rooms that allow them to step into a whole other world and close the door behind them.

Each girl I've had the opportunity to design a bedroom for has had a different type of dream. One girl dreamt of becoming a fashion designer so, for her, I created a room with a needle and thread that danced around the walls and a bed that accommodated bolts of fabric. For a girl who loved dolphins, I filled the bedroom with images that made it feel like one big aquarium. Even the tiles on the floor and her bedding looked like they were immersed in the ocean. Just find out what a young girl is crazy about and take that passion to the limit.

Siehera Thibodeau, as you can tell by looking at her room, is crazy about music. Sichera is a twelve-year-old with a loving heart. That heart just happens to have a hole in it, which has meant that she has

BELOW & OPPOSITE PAGE When you have dolphins swimming around your room, you don't need much else in the way of ornamentation.

had to endure four heart surgeries. During the last surgery, right before we came to her home, Siehera's kidneys failed and her lungs collapsed. Her condition is very serious and nobody is more aware of it than Siehera herself. While she was still in the hospital, we sat together and as I played the guitar, she sang a beautiful song she wrote in which she asks "Dear God" to tell her parents that she loves them.

In Siehera's old room, she had some posters of bands (Green Day is her favorite) with some butterfly cutouts tacked up on her walls. I just took that same idea and magnified it, creating bold, graphic, rock girl wallpaper with a backdrop of very girly butterflies and flowers. To create the wallpaper I took pictures of a friend of mine playing a bass guitar and singing into a microphone. I asked her to get outrageous and put some energy into it. I then downloaded the images

BELOW & OPPOSITE PAGE The most important thing in this room is what you don't see. We installed a HEPA (high efficiency particulate air) filter to help protect Siehera's fragile immune system from germs.

into my computer and handed it off to a custom wallpaper maker. The result was pretty outrageous!

That said, when you have something as wild and crazy as a larger-than-life chick rocking out on your walls, it's in your best interest to tone down the rest of the room. And that's what I did. The palette was limited to three colors—hot pink, black, and white—and all the furnishings kept fairly plain (though the white lacquer keeps them from looking *too* plain). As for the art, it's just a few guitars: great to look at and, if Siehera gets inspired, available for her to play.

And I really do hope that she gets inspired. Although the music of others brings her great joy (and she was completely wowed when I got her a guitar signed by Billy Joe Armstrong of Green Day), I was hoping that looking up from her bed and seeing a woman making music would motivate her to keep up with her own songs. I can't wait to be the guy in the front row at her concert checking out the band.

ABOVE You don't have to be a music lover to see the beauty in instruments hanging on the wall. Instead of stashing your guitar, flute, or tuba under the bed, consider displaying it as art.

OPPOSITE PAGE So you want to be a rock and roll star: Siehera has musical ambitions, but she's also still a little girl. Flowers, butterflies, and plenty of pink keep the vibe feminine.

Part III
Living Spaces

Have you ever walked into someone's living room and felt as though nobody really lives there? Where is the evidence of life? There's a reason living rooms are called living rooms: They're meant to be lived in! To my way of thinking, anything that falls into the realm of communal living spaces—whether you call it your living room, den, game room, entertainment room, playroom, or rec room—should be comfortable, not too formal, and reflective of your way of life. Live it up! Bring in the elements that represent the best aspects of your life—photographs, art, an awesome stereo, musical instruments, books, games—and you're going to have a room that you (and other people) are going to want to spend time in.

When you design the communal spaces in your home you're putting it all out there. You're letting other people know what your style is, what's important to you, how you spend your leisure time. But it's also all about what makes *you* feel relaxed and happy, so make it fit your needs. If you like to spread out and watch TV, make sure you buy a sofa that's long enough. If your kids like to lie on the rug and run through the DVD collection, concentrate on finding a great rug or non-itchy carpet. If you want to spend your time with your nose in a book, find a fantastic reading chair and reading lamp to put by its side. If you entertain a lot, create a furniture arrangement that will foster conversation. Really think about the purpose of the room you're creating— that's the key to making it functional as well as fun.

Go with the Flow

Feng shui is the Asian art of designing space to allow for the optimal flow of energy through the room. Some people believe in it, some people don't. **I think it's critical to consider flow when designing a room,** though I'm more concerned with the flow of traffic than the flow of energy. When you walk into a house and you have to step around a bookcase that juts out too far or you bump into a chair that's too close, it makes you feel unwelcome. But if a room is designed artfully, you'll feel as though you can kayak right through without running into any obstacles. You want your home to feel as though you can easily come in and out of each area and that every space is welcoming. That's flow.

When I designed my own home, I paid a lot of attention to flow, making sure to position the furniture so that each space feels open and easy to move through. I also took the idea one step further: While the rooms don't "match" per se, they flow together nicely. In other words, you don't feel as though you've stepped into a different house each time you go from one room to the next. Even though each room has its own purpose and personality, they mesh. You don't, for instance, go from a living room full of gorgeous wood craftsman furniture to a den filled with pop-arty plastic and acrylic pieces (but, hey, if you can figure out a way to make *that* transition work, go for it!).

The best examples are my living room and den. The living room is meant for quiet hanging out with friends and family. It's where I sometimes just sit (yes, I actually sit down once in a while) and read or play guitar. The den is my entertainment room. It's got a big TV and a great sound system. What the rooms basically have in common are furnishings that have a vintage '50s and '60s feel to them, even though it really is a mix between thrift store finds and pieces that I've made. But the majority of the upholstered pieces are low slung and you can see the beautiful grain in most of the wood furniture. And while the rooms don't have exactly the same color schemes, they share some of the same tones; they're just muted in the living room, brighter in the den.

Yet each room has a different function and is designed to let you know what that function is as soon as you walk in. If you have the luxury of having a

While you'd never call my living room (right) and my entertainment room (that's it on the opposite page) "matching," they harmonize. Both rooms have a lot of low to the ground furniture and share variations on the same colors.

living room that doesn't also double as a den/entertainment room, it's nice to create an environment that is conducive to sitting around and chatting. To that end, I arranged the furniture in this room to form sort of a conversation pit formed by a sofa and three chairs, nestled around a coffee table. The furniture is also arranged so that everyone can enjoy the fireplace; no chair has its back to the fire. It's a traditional arrangement that's traditional for a reason: It works.

The wood furniture pops against the backdrop of warm, neutral bamboo walls and floors. (Another advantage of floors made from light woods like bamboo, birch, or maple is that they hide dirt better than darker floors.) I also took care to inject my personality into this room without making any big, bold statements. The walls are hung with primarily small paintings, prints, and objects that were either thrift shop buys or created by myself or friends. The lamps are simple, made from found objects, and there are lots of guitars (and the errant surfboard) lying around. It's all about conversation and/or quiet time.

In many ways, the den/entertainment room shares the design sensibility of the living room, but it's turned way, way up—the bright orange coffee table alone screams that there's more of a party going on in here. This is the room where I can crank up the tunes or get rowdy with my buddies while watching a football game. But rather than creating a circular seating arrangement as I did in the living room, I gave this room an L-shaped arrangement so that the seating opens up to the entertainment center on the opposite wall. (I even designed the couch so that it's long enough for two people to lie across and watch TV at the same time.)

ABOVE Totem shelves are great for displaying art as well as books. To lean how to make one see page 218.

OPPOSITE PAGE The entertainment center deconstructed: instead of putting all your media equipment in a big, bulky cabinet, consider this airier, broken-up approach to storage.

In this room, everything is a little flashier. The artwork, paintings of animals that I did myself, are extra-large; the rug, made out of tiny pieces of old T-shirts, is ultra-fluffy; the throw pillows and vases are brightly colored, adding some punch to the mostly neutral surroundings; and many of the objects in the room—a light made out of faux leather that looks like a porcupine, sculptural stereo speakers—are as fun as they are functional. It's nice to have at least one room in the house that feels playful; for me, this is the grown-up equivalent of a kid's playroom. But it feels that way not because I've got a nice TV and stereo in there (grown-up toys), but because it's got energy and whimsy. And the key to that is letting color, art, and funny objects that catch your eye play a starring role.

ABOVE These chairs were a find at a school tag sale. The table's base came from a flea market, and I made the top myself. On the walls hang guitars from my collection; they're as beautiful as any art, at least to me.

OPPOSITE PAGE By propping art on the mantle piece in my living room I can easily swap it in and out. It's nice to change things around once in a while.

Use Flow to Create a Welcoming Entryway

To give your home flow, start at the beginning—that is, right in the entryway. The entryway often gets taken for granted and becomes just a place to toss keys and let mail pile up when it's thought of at all. I, on the other hand, think the entryway is the perfect place to introduce the overall style of your house and, more importantly, yourself. Here's a great opportunity to reveal a little bit about yourself to the people coming through the door.

For instance, the first thing you see when you walk into my house is an alcove painted ocean blue (a nod to the Pacific Ocean, which is just a few blocks away), a shelf tiled in earthy colors, and, hanging above it, a big sunburst that I crafted out of piano keys. The tile is a preview of things to come—I pick it up again on the living room fireplace—and the sunburst is a preview of, well, me. If you don't already know me and you walked in and saw that sunburst, you might be able to perceive that:

a) I like to make artwork out of old and found objects, b) I am "bursting" with energy, and c) I play the piano (actually, I don't play the piano very well but music *is* central to my life).

What you use to adorn your foyer doesn't have to be a metaphor for your life, but do put something meaningful there. It could be a family photo, or a painting of sunflowers, or a picture of Queen Elizabeth. Anything, as long as you love it. For one family of seven kids who had recently lost their dad, I took pictures of everyone and created a photo family tree that hung in the foyer. Beneath it is a candelabra I call the Tree of Light, which has a candle for both parents at the top and one for each child below. When you walk in the door of this family's home, you immediately get the importance of their family ties.

If you don't have a foyer and your front door opens up right into your living room, you probably won't be able to create a telling little design "sampler," but at the very least make sure that your entry is welcoming. Single out the first thing someone sees as she walks through the door and make it attractive. If it's the wall behind the couch, hang a striking piece of art; if it's a hall closet (unfortunately, some doors do open right in front of a hall closet), make sure the door to the closet is made of a beautiful type of wood or painted a striking color. If the front door opens right in front of the stairs, put a great runner on the steps or install an interesting banister.

Most important of all, be certain that your guests don't have to circumnavigate the back of a couch or chair to get into the room. Any obstacle to entering the house is unwelcoming. So, tempting as it is (especially if you have a small house or are a lover of furniture design, like me) to cram as many pieces of furniture into your home as possible, use restraint. Instead, keep the area inviting by keeping it open.

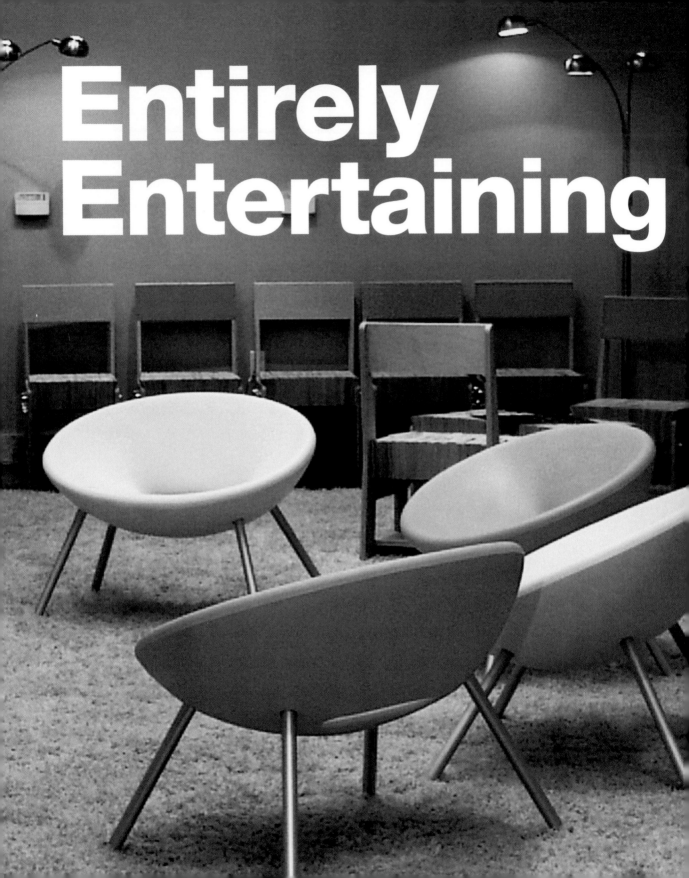

I've been in a few entertainment rooms that make you feel like you're on the lido deck of a cruise ship at four in the morning, listening to the ship's band play the same song for the tenth time. In other words, I've been in entertainment rooms that are not very entertaining. They make you feel as though you've walked into a bad rerun— or worse, a TV pilot that was so lousy it never aired. In my opinion **the room itself and not just what you watch or listen to inside of it should make you smile, laugh, have a good time.**

There are a couple surefire tactics you can use to create a fun room, and chief among them is color. Especially if you're creating a room that's going to be used by kids, choose colors that are vivid and lively for both the walls and the furniture. Try to keep the furnishings light: This isn't the time to haul out the old Louis XIV armoires and side tables. Instead, I recommend modern furnishings in clean-lined or even whimsical shapes. Bring in patterns and colors, too, to keep the mood light and kick-back comfortable.

On *EMHE* I had the opportunity to design two different entertainment rooms that, although they were not actually in homes (one was at a camp for critically and chronically ill children in Missouri, the other was at a center for homeless families in Colorado) have some ideas that translate well to the home. Both rooms are energetic and youthful, yet practical, too. They're all about good, clean (that is, easy to clean up) fun.

The furniture you put in a living room really says what the room is about. And in the case of the entertainment room I did for Camp Barnabas, I mean that literally. The camp was founded by a couple, Paul and Cyndy Teas, who cleaned out their savings and retirement accounts in order to create a place where sick kids could come and hike, ride horses, swim, and just be "normal" for a week. We renovated the Teas home, which, since they put everything they had into the camp, had been sorely neglected, as well as a few different parts of the camp.

I called the entertainment room the Silver Lining room because it was a place for the kids to go on rainy days. For that reason, I wanted it to be particularly bright and fun so that the kids didn't feel as though they were missing out. I also wanted it to be a casual room where everyone could lie around and be one big family. Anchored by a gi-normous TV, this room was all about television and, if there was any doubt, you need only look at the chairs and tables I made using old *TV Guides* and the *TV Guide*

ABOVE & OPPOSITE PAGE Old *TV Guides* that might have otherwise ended up in the recycling bin were bolted onto plywood to make these chairs. Up close this "wallpaper" looks like *TV Guide* covers with no rhyme or reason to their arrangement. Step back, and you can see their geometric pattern.

wallpaper. With their smooth plywood construction, the chairs and tables were created in the image of well-known modern pieces, but with a playfulness that's sometimes missing from pedigreed contemporary furniture. Depending on where you're standing, the wallpaper looks like *TV Guides* or like a fun patch of colors. That's because I was able to scan the cover images, then let my computer figure out how to arrange them into a pattern. When you're standing back from the wall, you can see there's a geometric method to the color madness.

It wasn't an accident that *TV Guides* played a big role in this room. *TV Guide* was good enough to put me on the cover and donate 10 percent of sales of that issue to Camp Barnabas, so we wanted to give them their due. And it was a great cause.

While there's nothing wrong with furnishing an entertainment room with lots of cushy couches and Barcaloungers, you can also go with lots of different chairs and floor pillows. Instead of a sofa in front of the TV, there's a semicircle of bright saucer chairs, and rather than a classic card table, there are groupings of *TV Guide* furniture. The room is also stocked with stacks of soft, fluffy floor pillows for the kids who can't walk to lie on and, underneath it all, a shaggy rug—the kind that makes you want to take your shoes off and walk barefoot.

Most entertainment rooms, especially those that are also used as game rooms and kids' playrooms, need plenty of storage, and Camp Barnabas's entertainment room was no exception. The storage piece I created for them is oversize, but so is the room. Anything smaller might look lost and lonely on the wall and, besides, this piece is eminently practical: Monopoly sets, checkerboards, DVDs, CDs, and all the other stuff that tends to clutter up entertainment rooms stays well hidden behind doors and within the baskets up top. Opposite, on the other side of the TV, two floating shelves balance out the main storage

RIGHT Not all entertainment rooms need to have a sofa. An assortment of chairs plus some floor cushions can do quite nicely (just make sure that you have enough of them).

piece, providing room for more stuff and flat surfaces to display pottery and other decorative items.

The combination of these elements—the funky furniture, the retro rug, and the unusual storage pieces—give the room personality. But what really makes it a place you want to hang out in is color. The citrusy assortment of orange, yellow, and lime keeps the tenor lighthearted. Note, though, that there are also a lot of whites and neutrals thrown into the mix to prevent color overkill. This balance keeps the room bright without turning it into a fruit bowl. The whole room gets a lift and, hopefully, everyone who enters gets a lift, too. I definitely had fun with the design, and the kids seemed to get into the fun aspect right away. I'll never forget the look on their faces when we opened the doors and let them in. "Ty, thank you so much!" "This is awesome!"

The other entertainment room shown on these pages was for an organization called Colorado Homeless Families. It's a great group that helps people get back on their feet. They already had a community center in place, but it was all white inside with little (make that no) personality. It needed color and lots of it.

This room serves several purposes. It's a place for families to watch movies and TV; for kids to play games, do homework and art projects; and for adults to use computers to look for jobs. So there's a lot going on, but color ties it all together. The "viewing" area, for instance, has a traditional arrangement of furniture (sofa, chair, coffee table), but the upholstered furnishings are bright, cheery, and covered with vibrant patterned pillows. The computer tables and chairs are made from simple plywood, but they too have a little color. We used a technique that involves using oil-based paint as a stain so that you still see the grain of the wood, but it has a pink or yellow or orange cast. It's actually very easy. All you do is thin the paint with paint thinner, brush it on the wood, then wipe it off with a cloth. The stain penetrates the wood and tints the grain.

The walls of this room are all about color, too. The mural I used here, though, lacks the symmetry

ABOVE & OPPOSITE PAGE Oil-based paint was thinned, brushed on, and then wiped off to stain these simple chairs and desks.

you usually find in rooms with motifs on the walls. And yet it works because the '60s-ish effusion of multihued circles, flowers, and the face of a young girl (all sort of a throwback to the Summer of Love) lends itself to randomness. Another reason is that the pops of color on the wall are balanced by the furniture in the room. There's no rule I can give you here—you'll just have to use your eye—but keep in mind that you don't want one area to be heavy with wall designs and furniture while another area is practically naked. In any case, if you're going to go for a random design, definitely experiment by taping up cutouts *before* you paint!

One of the advantages of community entertainment rooms is that there is usually ample space. But if you don't have the luxury of extra square footage in your own home, look at it as a test of your creativity. There are more ways to get around space limitations than you think. One room that proves it is a game "salon" I did for the Harvey family in Florida. A lot of the furniture in this room does double duty as storage space, which is one way to make the space you do have go further.

I should note that the Harveys, a family of six, were used to living in close quarters. When we met

ABOVE The mural's finishing touch was the beautiful face of a little girl who was among the people at the homeless facility we were helping. She was just the light of everyone's life, and now her face is lighting up the community center.

OPPOSITE PAGE Kicking back in a modPod chair with built-in speakers.

them, they had been residing all cramped up together in an old, dilapidated army barrack home in need of repairs. The father, Willie, had been trying to fix it up when he was diagnosed with epilepsy. This is particularly bad luck when your profession requires the operation of heavy machinery. He lost his job because his employers were afraid that he would have seizures while working. The mom was already working two jobs *and* putting herself through nursing school. They were still having a hard time getting by.

Yet for all their troubles and forced togetherness, the Harveys are a very warm and close family. I thought it would be nice for them to have a little room where they could enjoy each other's company (this time, by choice). The room was sort of an adjunct to the living room, and I filled it with a ton of games: jigsaw puzzles, Scrabble, chess, checkers, jacks, playing cards, marbles, Uno, Chinese checkers. You name it. But if there was any question about what the room was for, you only had to look up at the walls, one of which was painted with a puzzle pattern, another of which sports a gigantic maze blown up and framed.

The real beauty of this room, though, is the space-saving furniture. I created a series of 18-inch-by-18-inch cubes as well as some 18-inch-by-36-inch rectangles, which can be used as needed: stacked up for storage when the room is not in use, pulled down to function as tables and stools when it is. For more seating, I also designed some low benches that, because they're the same height, tuck in neatly next to the storage/seating units. Placing them against the wall maximized the open floor space, and they only need a few pillows placed on top to make them as comfy as a couch (well, almost).

When you're working with a small space (this one was about 10 feet by 10 feet), it's especially important to measure, measure, measure. Go into it knowing exactly how much space you have to work with and you'll have a much easier time creating a space that's neither too cluttered nor too stark—in other words, a space that's just right.

ABOVE & OPPOSITE PAGE This isn't just a room where you can do puzzles; the room itself is a puzzle, with interlocking pieces (the cubes and benches) that work for both storage and seating.

In Neutral Gear

I'm not usually called quiet, but I've been known to design a mellow room or two. What these rooms generally have in common is that they are built around neutral tones, mostly neutral wood tones. (As you've undoubtedly figured out by now, I am a wood connoisseur. I just love being able to see clearly the grains of wood, and I love a mix of complementary woods in one room.) There are a lot of ways to do neutral rooms—sticking to whites, creams, and off-whites, for example— **but I personally like to focus on the neutral beauty of wood.**

That was the case when I designed a living room for a man named Eric Hebert, a bachelor who suddenly found himself the father of eight-year-old twins. The kids, a boy and girl, were the children of Eric's sister, who died suddenly of heart disease at the age of thirty-seven. (Eric's parents had also died of the disease when he was a teenager.) So Eric moved from Montana to Idaho and took on the job of parenting his niece and nephew. They'd been living with their mom in a dilapidated trailer and, while Eric moved them out of there quickly, he couldn't do much better. He could only afford a "berm house," a partially underground basement type structure. They were all living there (along with all the spiders and other bugs taking shelter in the house) when we came along and built them a brand-new house.

Eric is this awesome guy who really stepped up to the plate when the kids had no one else to turn to, and I thought his new living room should reflect the "grown-up" decision he made. While I didn't want to make the room too serious—or forget that two kids were going to be hanging out in there—I wanted to make it look like it belonged to a mature adult. And, as Eric proved, he is definitely an adult.

Unlike most rooms I do, this one didn't have any big hits of color. There's still pop—for instance, the white pottery pops off the wood and the dark furniture pops off the lightly colored floor—but the room is for the most part subdued. Yet it's not dreary. One reason is that the materials used in this room have a very natural feel. The rich dark wood furniture and blond flooring used as a wall covering make the room feel as earthy as the Idaho terrain outside its doors. We also brought in other natural elements like tree branches, sculptures in organic forms, lightly tinted landscape photos, and even a small tree.

One rule of thumb to remember when you're doing a room in neutrals is to vary the tones or risk ending up with a dull space. While the wood

ABOVE The beauty of shelves is that they let you show off interesting objects, but that doesn't mean they can't be interesting objects in and of themselves.

OPPOSITE PAGE Brown and black are a great combination, just be wary of making a room look too drab. Here, surrounded by light walls and flooring, they pair up (and pop out) nicely.

pieces are all in the same dark tones, we went lighter for the sofas, the rug, and the floor. This way there's a good mix and the room feels warm and inviting.

This living room was also designed to fulfill a couple of functions. It's the place where the family can entertain and just hang out and talk *and* the room where they can watch TV. Flat-screen TVs fit pretty nicely over a fireplace, but in this case I purposely put the TV on the opposite wall so that if they look one way it feels like an entertainment room and if they look the other way it feels like a cozy room for hanging out by the fire. That, my friends, is known as maximizing your options!

ABOVE Creating balance and symmetry in a room doesn't mean that, if folded in half, one side of the room would lie perfectly on top of the other. The television is flanked by a cabinet on one side and a shelf on the other. They're not carbon copies of each other, but because they're the same height and all the pieces are made of the same dark stained wood, there is balance and harmony.

OPPOSITE PAGE Neutral doesn't necessarily mean devoid of color. The muted aqua on the walls here warms up the rooms but keeps the feeling light.

Room Accessorizing (and the Power of Three)

All the little items on display in your house, whether they're books, candles, shells, or a collection of porcelain dolls from the '50s, say something about you. They tell a story (and let's be honest, sometimes it's a bizarro story) about what you love. I find living rooms without any accessories puzzling: What, I always wonder, is this person all about?

Okay, so you need to fill your home with accessories that you love, but that is not the same as having hundreds of little tchotchkes lying around. Good design is more subtle than that. When it comes to accessorizing a room, you'll have better results if you go for quality. A beautiful handcrafted bowl, yes. The clay bowl you made in second grade, no. Also rein in the quantity. I'm all for collections—as I've said, I have many myself—but when you display thirty, forty, or fifty of something, chances are you're crossing the line into tchotchke territory. If you do have a vast collection and really want to display it in whole, think about using a "dedicated" glass case rather than crowding your collection onto open shelves.

Better yet, place small groupings of objects around the room. I generally group things in threes. In fact, looking back at photographs of rooms I've designed and surveying my own home, I've found that I'm actually kind of obsessed with the number 3. Three vases here, three rows of colored glasses there, three scientific beakers, three candles, three framed photographs, three potted orchids, three sand dollars… you get the picture. So here's a good rule of thumb for accessorizing: As Mies van der Rohe said, less is more. And as he might well have added, three is perfect.

The Everything Room

I love reading about homes that have a separate room for just about everything. The screening room. The billiard room. The music room. The workout room. The meditation room. The gift wrapping room. (*The gift wrapping room?*) What a great luxury to have a separate room for just about anything you like to do. But let's talk about real life. Most people have to make do with one or two multipurpose living spaces, rooms I call **"everything rooms."** Typically an everything room is a room where you can throw a cocktail party, hang out and watch old movies, play music, do homework, make art, and, yes, wrap gifts.

There's a couple of ways to create an everything room. More to the point, there's the bad way—crowding the room with couches and card tables, slapping down a treadmill in front of the TV, and calling it a day—and there's the good way, which involves working toward a more attractive solution. And as an overall rule of thumb, you can achieve that more attractive solution by combining both informal and formal furnishings. That may sound like a recipe for disaster, but I can show you a few examples of how that unlikely mix can actually turn out very well.

The first is a room I call the "Lion's Den." I designed it for Victor Marrero, the victim of two heart attacks, the second of which left him so disabled that he had to leave his job as a forklift operator. Victor is a single dad who has been raising his five sons, ages fifteen to twenty, by himself since their mother left twelve years ago. The family lives in Camden, New Jersey, a place where most people struggle to get by and crime is a serious problem. So Victor had had his work cut out for him making sure that his sons didn't fall victim to drugs and violence. And he's done a great job. These five guys are terrific kids, and, while I have met a lot of families, I have never met one as tightly knit as the Marrero family. They are like a football team. Victor has also helped out other parents by starting a group called Single Fathers of Camden to offer advice and support to dads.

When I asked Victor what would have happened to his kids if he hadn't been so vigilant, he said it would have been like throwing them into the lion's den. So I came to think of the living room that I designed for them as a different kind of lion's den—a place where the six of them could gather and stay safe. Victor had always tried hard to entertain the boys with charades, Scrabble, and other games, so an entertainment center with lots of storage was central to the design of the room. But this would also be their everything room, the place where they could entertain and just hang out as a family, so it needed to have a sense of warmth and light, too.

OPPOSITE PAGE I gave the idea of the "Lion's Den" a literal interpretation, papering the walls with a royal lion motif.

Because this was a family of men, I could easily have gone with all the typical male furnishings in browns and dark leather, but I chose white and orange instead: white to reflect that the family was making a clean start (and I mean that in the truest sense of the word—their dingy old furniture was so infested with bugs we had to burn it), and orange to keep the room young and hip. After all, it was going to be inhabited by five boys and one very cool dad.

Shelby Pope is a thirteen-year-old girl with polymorphic light eruption, a disease that makes her allergic to sunlight. She isn't able to go outside or even sit beside an uncovered window without having

ABOVE AND OPPOSITE PAGE Orange as an accent color keeps this room young. Even the orange shag rug—a '70s nightmare made hip again—looks cool.

her skin covered, so until we gave the family a new Shelby-friendly house, she had spent much of her time in a dark, tiny bedroom.

My job was to turn an old barn into a place for the whole family to gather and, after circumstances demanded it, their own private wine bar. The Popes live right in the heart of wine country and, as it turns out, instead of bringing over brownies or an apple pie to be neighborly, the people in this neck of the woods show friendship by making an offering of wine. During the short time we were in town making over the Pope home, the whole community came out toting along bottle after bottle. The family ended up with quite a collection and, well, we had to put all that wine somewhere.

Since the setting for this everything room was a barn, I kept the feel of the room rustic by using a lot of fairly rough recycled materials. For instance, old weathered wood I found in the barn was cut

BELOW When life gives you wine, build wine racks.

OPPOSITE PAGE The glazed straw-yellow walls behind the bar give the old barn a Tuscan feel and the room a golden glow.

into strips and turned into wainscoting. We gave the structure a new roof and its previous one of corrugated tin became the base of the bar (the top is recycled tile). Five old French oak wine barrels were propped against the wall purely because they looked very cool.

But I also juxtaposed the rougher stuff with a classic leather sofa and matching chairs as well as some antique pieces that, while not fancy, are far more formal than the tin bar. The mix of casual and more refined pieces makes the room a really impressive place to throw a party but keeps it from feeling stuffy. The family is still going to feel comfortable kicking back on the cozy cluster of furniture around the coffee table, throwing their feet up and watching a game on TV (there's a set in the antique armoire).

ABOVE The wine barrels, just for show, telegraph the message that good vintages are appreciated here.

OPPOSITE PAGE When you have the luxury of a lot of space, carving out intimate areas like this sitting arrangement makes the room seem more hospitable.

Part IV
Working Spaces

Does your work space work? Your livelihood may depend on it. Okay, nobody can say for sure whether having a comfortable, good-looking work space can increase your productivity, but I for one fall into the camp that believes a great space can give your work a boost. And considering that most people spend almost as much time in their offices as they do in their living rooms, it just makes sense to give your work space a look you love.

Even if it's mostly devoted to the daily grind, the space you work in ought to have an element of fun. Since I'm on the road so much, my office is my laptop, but I do have a work space at home that I've tried to instill with a sense of humor. On one wall I have a very large painting of a Japanese guy

karate chopping the top off a bottle. It reminds me to approach my work with power and precision.

While you probably have your nose in your work most of the time, there are going to be those moments when you look up and stare at the walls. Maybe it's while you're brainstorming, maybe it's while you're on the phone, maybe it's while you're taking a break. No matter what the reason—you deserve something great to look at. Make your work space aesthetically pleasing, and make it a place that enables you to get organized easily. A space that's orderly and attractive is going to make you feel like you can succeed at whatever you're doing. Work, after all, is work and sometimes we all need a little inspiration to keep cranking it out.

Clean & Simple

Some people believe that they actually think better in a messy office. I'm not one of them. When things are neat and well organized, my thinking is better organized, too. That's why **I'm a fan of offices that are fairly simple and make it easy to put things where they belong** (or at least let you shove things out of sight for awhile).

f there was ever a family that needed a clean and simple office, it was the Kibes, who run a family farm in Iowa. Farming is a messy business—believe me, after working on that project, I had the crusty boots to prove it—so their office needed to be an orderly place where the Kibes could get away from the mess and focus on the commercial side of their enterprise. The design of the space mirrors the rural nature of the business, yet many features of the office could work well in any home work space.

The five Kibes moved from the city to the country, intending to escape the bad influence of urban life on the kids and to fulfill the dream of Shawn, their father, who had always wanted to be a farmer. But there was a huge glitch. Not long after the family

ABOVE Wavy shelves give this otherwise standard storage unit a little personality. Look for furniture with out-of-the-ordinary lines.

OPPOSITE PAGE The desk in this office is clean-lined and simple in keeping with the goal of creating a retreat from the muck out on the farm.

ABOVE Galvanized steel lamps capture the rustic nature of the business but look chic and modern, too.

OPPOSITE PAGE Old farm machinery parts were scattered around the office to give it a country feel.

FOLLOWING SPREAD While you don't have to go to the extreme of turning a favorite photo into wallpaper, blowing up a picture so that it's way larger than expected lends drama to a room. Nobody who walks into this office is going to forget those cows anytime soon.

moved, their house burned down (a few days before Christmas, no less) and they were forced to live out of a trailer, with the kids sometimes sleeping in tents. Things got so bad that the Kibes had to sell the cattle they depended on for their small income. That was especially heartbreaking for the kids, who'd helped nurse and raise the animals since birth.

EMHE built a new house and barn for the family; my job was to design their office. When you walk into the space, you pretty much know that you're on a farm (either that or entering the office of someone with a weird cow fetish). Instead of just putting generic art in an office, I thought, why not put something that illustrates what the business is all about? So I took photographs of the farm's new cows, gave the images

a sepia tone on my computer, and had them turned into wallpaper. Shawn, a big guy who wasn't much for showing his feelings, got very emotional when he walked into the office for the first time and saw the cows. It was obvious how much his work meant to him, and it was a great feeling to help him get a new lease on life.

The rest of the office is very practical. There's a clean-lined table that acts as a desk and a few comfy chairs for visitors or for Shawn when he takes a break. Instead of going with traditional file cabinets, I found galvanized steel chests that look a little less formal but are just as storage-friendly. The light fixtures are also galvanized, and, since they look like something you might find in a barn, feel right at home next to the giant herd of cattle on the wall.

For more storage, I built a low plywood unit with curved shelves, then filled them with painted tins and galvanized buckets. You can find these at hardware, garden, and specialty stores and they're a terrific place to toss paperwork and office paraphernalia, from pens and pencils to mailing materials. One thing you might notice about this room is that it's done in primarily warm, earthy neutrals. Usually, I'd be inclined to add some color to such a neutral room to give it some pop, but this time I just decided to let the cows do all the talking. When a room's got several tons of bovine beauty staring out from the walls, it probably has enough punch already.

LEFT In some ways, this office does double duty. It's a place where farm business is conducted, and it's a place where the farmer can come in from the heat (or cold), take a load off, and relax for the few spare minutes he has in a day.

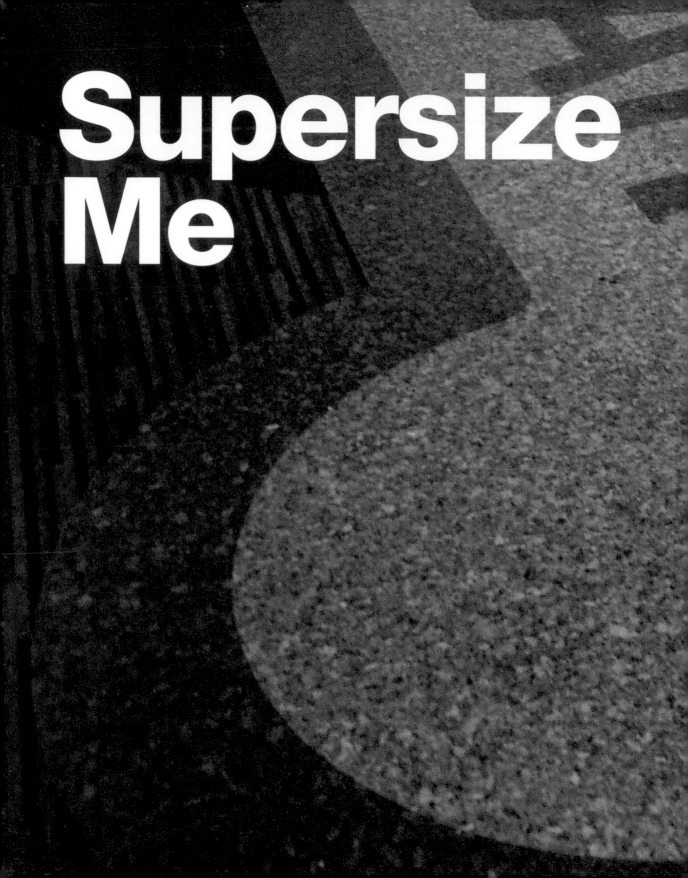

Supersize Me

There's one thing most home offices have in common: They're relatively small. For some reason, we tend to give ourselves lots of space for living and less space for work. But no worries: **You can do a lot with a little if you think strategically.**

ABOVE Want a llama for your mama? Giving photos of all the cute animals up for grabs in a prominent display was intended to expedite their adoption.

OPPOSITE PAGE Aqua and olive inject some playfulness into this office, but the colors aren't so wild as to look unprofessional. Cork, the material I used for this floor, is a renewable resource *and* easy on the feet.

The office on these pages may not look that small, but considering that it needed to accommodate a couple of workers as well as their clients, it's not all that spacious—especially when you consider that some of the clients coming in and out of the office are dogs, cats, and even the stray chicken or pig. I designed this space for the DeAeths, a family that runs an animal rescue operation out of their Texas home. Moved by the plight of so many abused and abandoned animals, the DeAeths began taking them in and caring for them before trying to place them in loving homes. The place was just crazy with dogs, cats, horses, and other assorted animals (including some rescued from Hurricane Katrina).

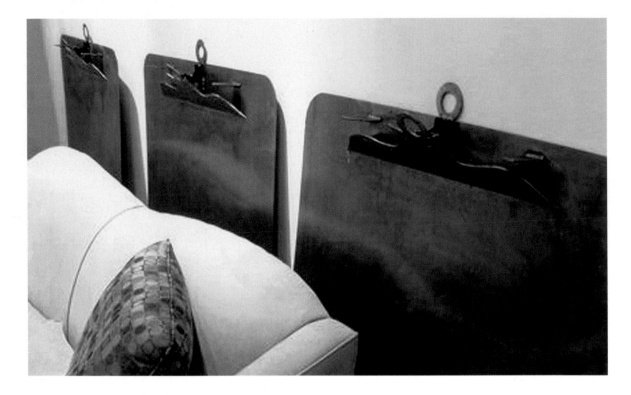

Meanwhile, their house became so neglected it was literally falling down around them.

As the nonprofit business they created—True Blue Animal Rescue (T-BAR)—grew, the DeAeths needed to get organized and present a more professional face to the public. Let's just say it was time they stopped conducting the operation out of boxes. The office had to provide ample storage for all the paperwork involved in animal adoption (and if you've ever tried to adopt a pet, you probably know that the application is as thick as a book), and help them keep the animals' comings and goings straight. I also thought the office should be bright and cheery. The lives of some of the animals had been really dreary, but now they were on the road to loving homes, so I wanted T-BAR's work space to reflect the happiness that awaited both the animals and their new owners.

And all this, of course, had to be accomplished within limited parameters. Luckily, I knew some

ABOVE To give you some idea of how big these clipboards are (see how I used them to display art on page 195), they are quite a bit taller than a sofa.

OPPOSITE PAGE Wall-hung cabinets, recessed lighting, and an apparatus for hanging little shelves and things frees up desk space.

space-saving strategies. The desks, for instance, are relatively narrow leaving a comfortable amount of floor space. Yet despite their slimness, they're relatively uncluttered because a panel on the wall behind them holds files and other objects that might ordinarily sit on the desk. Wall-hung metal and glass cabinets and drawers that slipped neatly underneath the desk gave the office plenty of storage without sacrificing any more floor space.

While it's easy to find office furniture in boringly institutional taupe, gray, and black, I urge you to go the extra mile and look for pieces that have some color. A lot of companies make metal furniture in a variety of shades. Those pieces make a room. Hanging some really simple but vibrant art on the wall can also go a long way toward livening up the office and making it feel less like a dungeon of drudgery. Here, for instance, I created some oversized (2' × 3') metal clipboards, and clipped on some photographs I manipulated using my computer. I also hung regular-size clipboards (the kind you can get at any office supply store) on the wall, which T-BAR uses to display pictures of the animals available for adoption. Clipboards, though, can be used for any kind of art display and are especially great for rotating the stream of drawings that kids bring home from school.

Just like office furniture, office floors needn't be drab. For the DeAeths, I created flooring made out of three colors of cork with a paw print and bone design (now their logo). Cork is a great choice for flooring not only because it's a renewable resource (they scrape the cork off the tree, then it grows back), but also because it's smooth, durable, and easy to clean, something you want in a floor that's going to be trod on by animals.

Last I heard, True Blue Animal Rescue was thriving, and I hope that having a well-appointed office has helped make the business run better. The DeAeths have been a bright spot in the lives of so many animals; they deserved a work space that could be a bright spot in theirs.

OPPOSITE PAGE Clipboards, big and small, are a great way to "frame" art.

Industrial Revolution

I have a lot of hobbies. I like to make art. I play music. I build furniture. I tinker around and fix things. Then there's my work. I have fabric samples, paint chips, and all kinds of paraphernalia related to the rooms I design for *EMHE* and my line of home fashions for Sears. Basically, that means that I have a lot of stuff, and it drives me crazy if I can't find what I'm looking for. You, too? Organization, my friends. That's the answer. Organization. And for that you might take a page from **how some industrial-type spaces are designed.**

This brings me to Kevin Nutsch's auto shop, a work space that is a great example of how to make sure that everything has its place. In this particular case, I used bins (and bins and more bins) to give a state-of-the-art garage some clutter control, an idea that can be applied almost anywhere, whether it be in a kitchen, a crafts room, or a home office.

Kevin was in need of a new auto shop because the one he had, which was right next to his home, was irrevocably damaged when a propane leak caused his house to explode. Thankfully, Kevin, his wife, and their five daughters were on vacation at the time, but the explosion destroyed everything, including their livelihood.

While the rest of the team toiled away on creating a new house for the family, I worked on Kevin's garage. On one wall, I built shelving designed to hold forty-eight bins, enough so that all the auto parts Kevin works with can be housed separately—no more digging through boxes to find what he was looking for. For good measure, I also built more bin storage into the worktables (which are on wheels so they can easily be moved around the shop). To keep little parts like nuts, bolts, and screws organized, I created a storage unit made from paint cans attached to a sheet of plywood. This is a really easy and cheap way to create storage space, and if you group the cans closely together, the whole unit looks like a piece of wall art. Anything can go inside the cans: yarn and needles if you're a knitter, kids' art supplies, toys, kitchen utensils.

Now fix-it garages aren't exactly glamorous places, but I didn't see any reason why Kevin's shop shouldn't have some drama. Taking my cue from some rusting

LEFT Rows of cans bolted to a board help keep odds and ends organized. Shiny cans are a lot better looking than old rusted cans so get the newest-looking ones you can find.

OPPOSITE PAGE Shelves with built-in cubbyholes and bins are a great storage solution for any room.

FOLLOWING SPREAD This auto shop is a combination of shiny and rusted out—just like a lot of cars.

autos sitting outside the shop, I painted the walls with a metallic paint sprayed with an oxidizer to create instant rust. To echo the wall's fiery tones, I painted the tables with bright orange automotive paint. The shiny surface looks cool and, more importantly, is easy to clean.

If you spend a lot of time in your work space, whether it's doing work that's your livelihood or work that's simply a passion, do yourself a favor and make it more than just functional. Even if the space is industrial, give it some character, make it interesting, or as in the case of a garage/woodworking shop I did for a guy named Gordon Harrison, make it beautiful.

Gordon is a man after my own heart. He loves working with wood and was about to switch careers and become a cabinetmaker when he was diagnosed with pancreatic cancer. This is a guy who was known in the neighborhood as someone who wouldn't hesitate to stop what he was doing to help you out if you needed something done to your house. Even when he was undergoing chemotherapy, he spent time plotting ways to help a neighbor family remodel their kitchen, enlisting the help of other neighbors in the community and even getting donations from vendors. (Sound

familiar?) This extraordinary act of kindness at such a dire, scary time in his life led his neighbors to contact us so that they could return the favor.

I knew that having an incredible woodworking shop would mean a lot to Gordon and that he, like me, really appreciates the beauty of wood. Taking that as my cue, I created a wall installation made up of just about every type of wood I could find: mahogany, zebra wood, blood wood, walnut, ash, birch—you name it. I simply cut the wood into geometric shapes and mounted them on the wall with a nail gun. It's like one giant wood collage, no artistry needed because the wood itself is so beautiful. Of course, I also dealt with the more practical side of things by outfitting the shop with all new tools and moveable carts so he could take some of his work outside or put the carts into his truck.

My favorite part of the shop are the hand-carved mahogany doors. Since the space is all about the amazing things you can do with wood, it seemed appropriate that the entrance show how elegant woodworking can get. It was appropriate, too, that a guy who'd done so much for others would now have the means to do something for his own family.

OPPOSITE PAGE AND FOLLOWING SPREAD Most people long for an organized garage; I believe in an organized and beautiful garage, especially if you're going to be working in it. Here, the artwork is a collage of gorgeous hardwoods, perfect for a woodworker.

Oh, and One More Thing...

I hope these words, pictures, and stories have shown you that, yes, there is a method to the madness that goes on at *Extreme Makeover: Home Edition*. Honestly, sometimes it is crazy madness trying to do what we do in the amount of time that we have to do it. But this is without a doubt the most rewarding job I will ever have. I have learned so much and met so many amazing people. Their stories have inspired me beyond measure, and I hope that, by passing them on, I've helped to inspire you, too.

Take some of the ideas I've given you and think of not only what you can do to your own place, but also what you can do to somebody else's. Get out there and get your hands dirty. What I've seen on the job is that when good people come together to do something and make a difference, incredible things can happen. **Use good design to rock your world. I know it can be done; I see it happen every week.** Now I'm going to get going because I've still got a lot of people to meet and a lot of rooms to design—and I can't wait to get to it!

Appendix
Build
Your Own
Furniture

If you've never picked up a hammer in your life, these three do-it-yourself projects may be a little daunting. They're not difficult, but some experience may be required. That said, they offer a great opportunity to learn about woodworking if you can find someone to show you the ropes. Start asking around; **chances are you'll find someone who's dying to get his or her hands on a miter saw.**

Stacked Bench

One day I was staring at a pile of Baltic birch plywood (now you know how I spend my free time) when it occurred to me that the edges of the plywood had some really striking features. In case you didn't know, Baltic birch (sometimes called Russian birch) is a special type of plywood that's used for making furniture and other things that require strength and stability. It's not necessarily more expensive than regular plywood, but it might not be available at your local mega hardware store. You might need to look at a place that specializes in hardwood.

It's worth the extra legwork, though. Most plywood only has five plies (plies are individual $1/32$" to $1/16$" planks of wood that are layered together in cross-grained stacks), but Baltic birch has seven or more. The other thing about Baltic birch is that, while most plywood has knotholes or voids in some of the plies, Baltic birch plywood is fabricated with all the knotholes or voids filled or plugged. This last bit of sage plywood arcana is what led me to my little design epiphany. Have I confused you yet? Stay with me, people.

Anyway, instead of laying the plywood flat as you'd expect, I decided to stack the pieces in such a way that the edges would be exposed on the top and sides of the bench. It involved a little math to get the dimensions right, but I've got it all figured out and I'm passing on the instructions to you.

Wood you'll need:

Bench Top

12 pieces of Baltic birch plywood, which you'll cut to 22" long by 2" wide each

11 pieces of Baltic birch plywood, which you'll cut to 18" long by 2" wide each (you want to actually make these a hair shorter than 18" long, which I'll explain in a minute)

Bench Legs

24 pieces of Baltic birch plywood, which you'll cut to 16" long by 2" wide each (again, on these, make them a hair shorter than 16" long)

22 pieces of Baltic birch plywood, which you'll cut to 18" long by 2" wide each

Pretty simple so far. The reason those pieces need to be a hair shorter, is so that when you do the final assembly the slats extend a little "proud" on your lap joints. At the end, you can sand it all flush.

Tools & other stuff you'll need:

Table saw

Carpenter's wood glue

Assembly hammer (rubber mallet)

Sandpaper

Polyurethane (optional)

Clamps

Brad nailer (optional)

Now for the fun part:

1. Cut your wood to size with a table saw and make sure all your edges are clean of any "fuzz" from cutting. Then start stacking.

We'll make the bench in 3 pieces, then assemble the 3 pieces last for the final product.

For the top:

2. Work on a flat surface and keep a good straightedge handy. Start with one of your long pieces. Apply a light coat of glue across its surface. Apply glue to a shorter piece's surface, then carefully stack them so that the long and short pieces create "fingers" of equal length on each side. Continue alternating lengths on top of one another.

It's okay to use some tiny nails from a brad nailer (a nail gun) to hold the pieces together as you work, but you'll still need to use a couple of clamps to hold the pieces together while they dry.

For the sides:

3. Do each side the same way you did the top, except start with a short length first. This time, make sure the pieces are flush on one end as you stack; you only want fingers at the top.

Stacked Bench, continued

Putting it all together:

4. Carefully put glue on the inside of the "fingers" one side at a time. Be sparing with the glue; it will get messy if you're not careful. It helps to use a small paintbrush. Work fast or the glue will start to stick before you can begin assembly. (If you'd prefer a more relaxed pace, consider buying extended "open" time glue, which doesn't dry as fast.) Once you get glue on the gluing surfaces for one side go ahead and assemble. The fingers will fit tight, so you may need to tap it together with an assembly hammer.

5. Make sure your sides are square to the top, and let the glue set. If you cut the short pieces a hair short, then your fingers should protrude a little bit on the top and sides.

6. Sand the fingers flush, give it a final sanding, and apply a finish. I like to brush on polyurethane (available at any home center; get the kind that's water cleanup). You'll need to put on a couple of coats because the exposed plywood edges will suck it up at first. Do it right and you'll have a beautiful and practical piece for your pad.

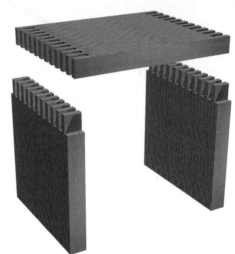

Veneer Shade Lamp

I created this lamp way back during the first season of the show. A couple pieces of yellow pine and a scrap of veneer were the inspiration. You can use whatever type of wood and veneer you want; for my lamp I used yellow pine for the legs, poplar for the cross members, and a piece of maple veneer for the shade.

Wood you'll need:

4 pieces walnut, which you'll cut to 1¼" wide by 8" tall by ¾" thick, plus a few extra pieces in case you mess up

2 pieces contrasting colored wood (such as maple), which you'll cut to 10" long by ¾" wide by ¾" thick, plus a few extra pieces in case you mess up

1 piece veneer, 27" by 8"

Tools you'll need:

Table saw

Stacked dado cutter or sliding miter saw

Band saw or jigsaw

Masking tape or a few small clamps

Carpenter's wood glue

1. Start by milling the leg pieces and crosspieces to size. Take your time and make sure your cuts are straight and true. I suggest that you cut a couple extra legs and cross member pieces to aid you in your setup for the next steps.

2. Next you need to work on the joinery, the recessed spots where the pieces of wood will intersect. This step will drive you mad if you let it, so I recommend taking your time and making sure you have those extra pieces handy for setup, just in case you mess something up. Also, err on the side of milling away too little—it's easier to remove wood with a file or sandpaper than to fill.

3. First, mill the dados—slots—in the leg pieces where the cross members attach. There are a couple ways to do this. For the hard-core woodworker with the awesome shop, you can use a stacked dado cutter, but if you don't have one available, use a sliding miter saw. Most sliding miter saws have a stop setup where you can set the blade to cut a certain depth. In this case you need to cut ⅜" deep. Lay out your cut, and just nibble away at it until you have ¾" wide by ⅜" dado cut about 2" up from the bottom of the leg. When you have a dado cut in all 4 legs, take them over to the band saw or get out your jigsaw and cut a slot right down the middle about 4" down to accept the veneer shade. When finished with the leg pieces, you should have something that looks like this:

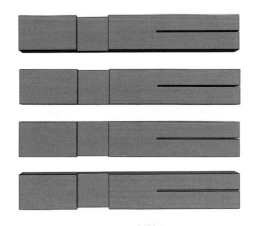

4. Now you're going to do the cross members. These are a little more difficult. You'll perform the same milling operations, with the same tools, but you do have to be careful to do each cut or dado on the correct face surface of the pieces to make it all work. First, do the half lap joint in the middle of the 2 cross members. Simply cut a ¾" dado ⅜" deep exactly in the middle of each of the two cross members so that they fit together and form a cross.

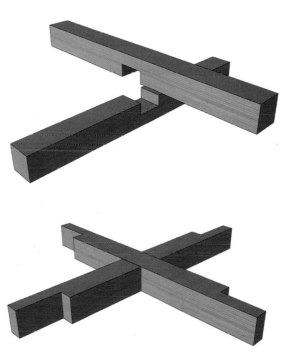

Veneer Shade Lamp, continued

That's easy enough. Now mill the ends so they fit into the dados in the legs. You'll need the other half of the half laps at each end. This can get tricky because you need a dado at each end of your cross member pieces (now stay with me here) on opposite sides. So basically you need a 1½" wide by ⅜" deep dado at each end of your cross member pieces.

Once you have your legs and cross members milled (or cut) your assembly looks something like this:

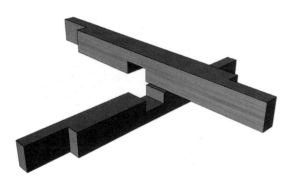

5. It's all downhill from here. Now it's time to assemble the base. Put wood glue on all your mating surfaces, being careful not to get too messy, and assemble your lamp base. If you've taken your time and cut your joinery correctly, then everything will be snug. Use clamps where needed, and do be sure all pieces are square to each other before the glue sets up.

6. Cut the veneer to make the shade. Carefully curl it into a tube and insert into the slots, making sure to insert the portion where it overlaps into one of the slots as well. It doesn't hurt to use a little glue where it overlaps and use masking tape or a small squeeze clamp to keep the exposed seam together until the glue sets up. You can buy the lamp socket and cord at your local home center and install according to directions. Insert a low-wattage bulb, and there you have it: a nice environment-friendly lamp for your place.

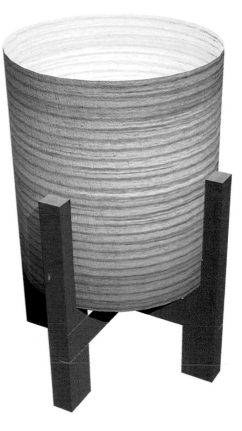

Totem Shelf

I'm a big fan of totem shelves. They aren't as bulky as regular bookshelves, so they're good for small spaces, plus they give you the opportunity to really spotlight the art and other collectibles you love.

Wood and metal you'll need:

1 8-foot-long, ¾"-thick, 11"-wide piece of hardwood (such as oak, cherry, or walnut)

1 8-foot-long 6-×-6-inch cedar post

3 × 3 × 3 angle bracket

cedar shims (wedgelike pieces of wood to fill in gaps)

Tools you'll need:

Dado blade, table saw or regular compound miter saw

¾" chisel

Assembly hammer (rubber mallet)

1. Using your dado blade, table saw or miter saw, cut a ¾" groove 2½ inches deep in the cedar post (16 inches on center), spacing every 16 inches.

2. If necessary, remove any remaining stubble inside groove with the chisel.

3. Using a compound miter saw or table saw, cut five 11-×-16-inch shelves out of the piece of hardwood.

4. Using a rubber mallet, hammer the 11-×-16-inch shelves into the ¾" grooves in the cedar post.

5. If there is any looseness between the shelves and the grooves, wedge cedar shims in the gaps. Score the shims lightly with a saw, then break them off where they come out of the grooves.

6. Now you're going to work on putting the whole thing together. Stand the post against the wall as close as possible; mark its top. Mount the angle bracket on the wall, ideally where there is a stud. (If there isn't, use drywall anchors.) Next, put the post in place under the top of the bracket and attach it with screws. If your floor is at all uneven, use a cedar shim to tighten the gap between the floor and the post.

This side is attached to the top of the post. Stand the post in place, mark the location of the top on the wall, install the angle bracket at that mark. Stand the post in place and attach it from the top with screws. (make sure it's plumb or level both ways)

This side is attached to the wall by screwing directly to a stud, or using good drywall anchors.

3"x3"x3" angle bracket available at most home centers (or something similar to it)

Index

Page numbers in *italics* refer to illustrations.